THE HOLLOW TREE AND DEEP WOODS PEOPLE

BY

ALBERT BIGELOW PAINE

D.

ALBERT BIGELOW PAINE

LITTLE JACK RABBIT AND BUNTY BUN

JACK RABBIT TELLS ABOUT HIS SCHOOL-DAYS,

AND WHY HE HAS ALWAYS

THOUGHT IT BEST TO LIVE ALONE

The Little Lady has been poring over a first reader, because she has started to school now, and there are lessons almost every evening. Then by and by she closes the book and comes over to where the Story Teller is looking into the big open fire.

The little lady looks into the fire, too, and thinks. Then pretty soon she climbs into the Story Teller's lap and leans back, and looks into the fire and thinks some more.

"Did the Hollow Tree people ever go to school?" she says. "I s'pose they did, though, or they wouldn't know how to read and write, and send invitations and things."

The Story Teller knocks the ashes out of his pipe and lays it on the little stand beside him.

"Why, yes indeed, they went to school," he says. "Didn't I ever tell you about that?"

"You couldn't have," says the Little Lady, "because I never thought about its happening, myself, until just now."

"Well, then," says the Story Teller, "I'll tell you something that Mr. Jack Rabbit told about, one night in the Hollow Tree, when he had been having supper with the 'Coon and 'Possum and the Old Black Crow, and they were all sitting before the fire, just as we are sitting now. It isn't really much about school, but it shows that Jack Rabbit went to one, and explains something else, too."

Mr. Crow had cooked all his best things that evening, and everything had tasted even better than usual. Mr. 'Possum said he didn't really feel as if he could move from his chair when supper was over, but that he wanted to do the right thing, and would watch the fire and poke it while the others were clearing the table, so that it would be nice and bright for them when they were ready to enjoy it. So then the Crow and the 'Coon and Jack Rabbit flew about and did up the work, while Mr. 'Possum put on a fresh stick, then lit his pipe, and leaned back and stretched out his feet, and said it surely was nice to have a fine, cozy home like theirs, and that he was always happy when he was doing things for people who appreciated it, like those present.

MR. RABBIT SAID HE CERTAINLY DID APPRECIATE BEING INVITED TO THE HOLLOW TREE

Mr. Rabbit said he certainly did appreciate being invited to the Hollow Tree, living, as he did, alone, an old bachelor, with nobody to share his home; and then pretty soon the work was all done up, and Jack Rabbit and the others drew up their chairs, too, and lit their pipes, and for a while nobody said anything, but just smoked and felt happy.

Mr. 'Possum was first to say something. He leaned over and knocked the ashes out of his pipe, then leaned back and crossed his feet, and said he'd been thinking about Mr. Rabbit's lonely life, and wondering why it was that, with his fondness for society and such a good home, he had stayed a bachelor so long. Then the Crow and the 'Coon said so, too, and asked Jack Rabbit why it was.

Mr. Rabbit said it was quite a sad story, and perhaps not very interesting, as it had all happened so long ago, when he was quite small.

"My folks lived then in the Heavy Thickets, over beyond the Wide Grasslands," he said; "it was a very nice place, with a good school, kept by a stiff-kneed rabbit named Whack—J. Hickory Whack—which seemed to fit him. I was the only child in our family that year, and I suppose I was spoiled. I remember my folks let me run and play a good deal, instead of making me study my lessons, so that Hickory Whack did not like me much, though he was afraid to be as severe as he was with most of the others, my folks being quite well off and I an only child. Of course, the other scholars didn't like that, and I don't blame them now, though I didn't care then whether they liked it or not. I didn't care for anything, except to go capering about the woods, gathering flowers and trying to make up poetry, when I should have been doing my examples. I didn't like school or J. Hickory Whack, and every morning I hated to start, until, one day, a new family moved into our neighborhood. They were named Bun, and one of them was a little girl named Bunty—Bunty Bun."

When Mr. Rabbit got that far in his story he stopped a minute and sighed, and filled his pipe again, and took out his handkerchief, and said he guessed a little speck of ashes had got into his eye. Then he said:

"The Buns lived close to us, and the children went the same way to school as I did. Bunty was little and fat, and was generally behind, and I stayed behind with her, after the first morning. She seemed a very well-behaved little Miss Rabbit, and was quite plump, as I say, and used to have plump little books, which I used to carry for her, and think how nice it would be if I could always go on carrying them and helping Bunty Bun over the mud-holes and ditches."

Mr. Rabbit got another speck of ashes in his eye, and had to wipe it several times and blow his nose hard. Then he said:

"She wore a little red cape and a pretty linsey dress, and her ears were quite slim and silky, and used to stand straight up, except when she was sad over anything. Then they used to lop down quite flat; when I saw them that way it made me sad, too. But when she was pleased and happy, they set straight up and she seemed to laugh all over.

"I forgot all about not liking school. I used to watch until I saw the Bun children coming, and then run out and get behind, with Bunty, and take her books, and wish there was a good deal farther to go. When it got to be spring and flowers began to bloom, I would gather every one I saw for Bunty Bun, and once I made up a poem for her. I remember it still. It said:

"Oh, Bunty Bun,
The spring's begun,
The violet's are in bloom.
Oh, Bunty Bun,
I'll pick you one,
All full of sweet perfume.

"The sun is bright,
Our hearts are light,
And we will skip and run.
Prick up your ears,
And dry your tears,
Dear bunny, Bunty Bun."

"Mr. Rabbit said he didn't suppose it was the best poetry, but that it had meant so much to him then that he couldn't judge it now, and, anyway, it was no matter any more. The other children used to tease them a good deal, Mr. Rabbit said, but that he and Bunty had not minded it so very much, only, of course, he wouldn't have had them see his poem for anything. The trouble began when Bunty Bun decided to have a flower-garden.

"She used to see new flowers along the way to and from school that she wanted me to dig up for her so she could set them out in her garden. I liked to do it better than anything, too, only not *going* to school, because the ground was pretty soft and sticky, and it made my hands so dirty, and Hickory Whack was particular about the children having clean hands. I used to hide the flower plants under the corner of the school-house every morning, and hurry in and wash my hands before school took up, and the others used to watch me and giggle, for they knew what all that dirt came from. Our school was just one room, and there were rows of nails by the door to hang our things on, and there was a bench with the wash-basin and the water-pail on it, the basin and the pail side by side. It was a misfortune for me that they were put so close together that way. But never mind—it is a long time ago.

"One morning in April when it was quite chilly Bunty Bun saw several pretty plants on the way to school that she wanted me to dig up for her, root and all, for her garden. I said it would be better to get them on the way home that night, but Bunty said some one might come along and take them and that she wouldn't lose those nice plants for anything. So I got down on my knees and dug and dug with my hands in the cold, sticky dirt, until I got the roots all up for her, and my hands were quite numb and a sight to look at. Then we hurried on to school, for it was getting late.

"When we got to the door I pushed the flower plants under the edge of the house, and we went in, Bunty ahead of me. School had just taken up, and all the scholars were in their seats except us. Bunty Bun went over to the girls' side to hang up her things, and I stuck my hat on a nail on our side, and stepped as quick as I could to the bench where the water was, to wash my hands.

"There was some water in the basin, and I was just about to dip my hands in when I looked over toward Bunty Bun and saw her little ears all lopped down flat, for the other little girl rabbits were giggling at her for coming in with me and being late. The boy rabbits were giggling at me, too, which I did not mind so much. But I forgot all about the basin, for a minute, looking at Bunty Bun's ears, and when I started to wash my hands I kept looking at Bunty, and in that way made an awful mistake; for just when the water was feeling so good to my poor chilled hands, and I was waving them about in it, all the time looking at Bunty's droopy ears, somebody suddenly called out, 'Oh, teacher, Jacky Rabbit's washing his hands in the water-pail! Jacky Rabbit's washing his hands in the water-pail, teacher!'

"And sure enough, I was! Looking at Bunty Bun and pitying her, I had made a miss-dip, and everybody was looking at me; and J. Hickory Whack said, in the most awful voice, 'Jack Rabbit, you come here, at once!'"

Mr. Rabbit said he could hardly get to Hickory Whack's desk, he was so weak in the knees, and when Mr. Whack had asked him what he had meant by such actions he had been almost too feeble to speak.

"I couldn't think of a word," he said, "for, of course, the only thing I could say was that I had been looking at Bunty Bun's little droopy ears, and that would have made everybody laugh, and been much worse. Then the teacher said he didn't see how he was going to keep himself from whipping me soundly, he felt so much that way, and he said it in such an awful tone that all the others were pretty scared, too, and quite still, all of them but just one—one scholar on the girls' side, who giggled right out loud—and I know you will hardly believe it when I tell you that it was Bunty Bun! I was sure I knew her laugh, but I couldn't believe it and, scared as I was, I turned to look, and there she sat, looking really amused, her slim little ears sticking straight up as they always did when she enjoyed anything."

Mr. Rabbit rose and walked across the room and back, and sat down again, quite excitedly.

"Think of it, after all I had done for her! I saw at once that there would be no pleasure in carrying her books and helping her over the mud-puddles in the way I had planned. And just then Hickory Whack grabbed a stick and reached for me. But he didn't reach quite far enough, for I was always rather spry, and I was half-way to the door with one spring, and out of it and on the way home, the next. Of course he couldn't catch me, with his stiff leg, and he didn't try. When I got home I told my folks that I didn't feel well, and needed a change of scene. So they said I could visit some relatives in the Big Deep Woods—an old aunt and uncle, and I set out on the trip within less than five minutes, for I was tired of the Thickets. My aunt and uncle were so glad to see me that I stayed with them, and when they died they left me their property. So I've always stayed over this way, and live in it still. Sometimes I go over to the Heavy Thickets, and once I saw Bunty Bun. She is married, and shows her age. She used to be fat and pretty and silly. Now she is just fat and silly, though I don't suppose she can help those things. Still, I had a narrow escape, and I've never thought of doing garden work since then for anybody but myself and my good friends, like those of the Hollow Tree."

MR. 'POSSUM'S SICK SPELL

MR. 'POSSUM HAS A NIGHT ADVENTURE

WHICH CAUSES EXCITEMENT

Once upon a time, said the Story Teller, something very sad nearly happened in the Hollow Tree. It was Mr. 'Possum's turn, one night, to go out and borrow a chicken from Mr. Man's roost, and coming home he fell into an old well and lost his chicken. He nearly lost himself, too, for the water was icy cold and Mr. 'Possum thought he would freeze to death before he could climb out, because the rocks were slippery and he fell back several times.

As it was, he got home almost dead, and next morning was sicker than he had ever been before in his life. He had pains in his chest and other places, and was all stuffed up in his throat and very scared. The 'Coon and the Crow who lived in the Hollow Tree with him were scared, too. They put him to bed in the big room down-stairs, and said they thought they ought to send for somebody, and Mr. Crow said that Mr. Owl was a good hand with sick folks, because he looked so wise and didn't say much, which always made the patient think he knew something.

So Mr. Crow hurried over and brought Mr. Owl, who put on his glasses and looked at Mr. 'Possum's tongue, and felt of his pulse, and listened to his breathing, and said that the cold water seemed to have struck in and that the only thing to do was for Mr. 'Possum to stay in bed and drink hot herb tea and not eat anything, which was a very sad prescription for Mr. 'Possum, because he hated herb tea and was very partial to eating. He groaned when he heard it and said he didn't suppose he'd ever live to enjoy himself again, and that he might just as well have stayed in the well with the chicken, which was a great loss and doing no good to anybody. Then Mr. Owl went away, and told the Crow outside that Mr. 'Possum was a very sick man, and that at his time of life and in his state of flesh his trouble might go hard with him.

So Mr. Crow went back into the kitchen and made up a lot of herb tea and kept it hot on the stove, and Mr. 'Coon sat by Mr. 'Possum's bed and made him drink it almost constantly, which Mr. 'Possum said might cure him if he didn't die of it before the curing commenced.

He said if he just had that chicken, made up with a good platter of dumplings, he believed it would do him more good than anything, and he begged the 'Coon to go and fish it out, or to catch another one, and try it on him, and then if he did die he would at least have fewer regrets.

But the Crow and the 'Coon said they must do as Mr. Owl ordered, unless Mr. 'Possum wanted to change doctors, which was not a good plan until the case became hopeless, and that would probably not be before some time in the night. Mr. 'Coon said, though, there was no reason why that nice chicken should be wasted, and as it would still be fresh, he would rig up a hook and line and see if he couldn't save it. So he got out his fishing things and made a grab hook and left Mr. Crow to sit by Mr. 'Possum until he came back. He could follow Mr. 'Possum's track to the place, and in a little while he had the fine, fat chicken, and came home with it and showed it to the patient, who had a sinking spell when he looked at it, and turned his face to the wall and said he seemed to have lived in vain.

Mr. Crow, who always did the cooking, said he'd better put the chicken on right away, under the circumstances, and then he remembered a bottle of medicine he had once seen sitting on Mr. Man's window-sill outside, and he said while the chicken was cooking he'd just step over and get it, as it might do the patient good, and it didn't seem as if anything now could do him any harm.

So the Crow dressed the nice chicken and put it in the pot with the dumplings, and while Mr. 'Coon dosed Mr. 'Possum with the hot herb tea Mr. Crow slipped over toMr. Man's house and watched a good chance when the folks were at dinner, and got the bottle and came back with it and found Mr. 'Possum taking a nap and the 'Coon setting the table; for the dinner was about done and there was a delicious smell of dumplings and chicken, which made Mr. 'Possum begin talking in his sleep about starving to death in the midst of plenty. Then he woke up and seemed to suffer a good deal, and the Crow gave him a dose of Mr. Man's medicine, and said that if Mr. 'Possum was still with them next morning they'd send for another doctor.

Mr. 'Possum took the medicine and choked on it, and when he could speak said he wouldn't be with them. He could tell by his feelings, he said, that he would never get through this day of torture, and he wanted to say some last words. Then he said that he wanted the 'Coon to have his Sunday suit, which was getting a little tight for him and would just about fit Mr. 'Coon, and that he wanted the Crow to have his pipe and toilet articles, to remember him by. He said he had tried to do well by them since they had all lived together in the Hollow Tree, and he supposed it would be hard for them to get along without him, but that they would have to do the best they could. Then he guessed he'd try to sleep a little, and closed his eyes. Mr. 'Coon looked at Mr. Crow and shook his head, and they didn't feel like sitting down to dinner right away, and pretty soon when they thought Mr. 'Possum was asleep they slipped softly up to his room to see how sad it would seem without him.

Well, they had only been gone a minute when Mr. 'Possum woke up, for the smell of that chicken and dumpling coming in from Mr. Crow's kitchen was too much for him. When he opened his eyes and found that Mr. 'Coon and Mr. Crow were not there, and that he felt a little better— perhaps because of Mr. Man's medicine—he thought he might as well step out and take one last look at chicken and dumpling, anyway.

It was quite warm, but, being all in a sweat, he put the bed-sheet around him to protect him from the draughts and went out to the stove and looked into the pot, and when he saw how good it looked he thought he might as well taste of it to see if it was done. So he did, and it tasted so good and seemed so done that he got out a little piece of dumpling on a fork, and blew on it to cool it, and ate it, and then another piece, and then the whole dumpling, which he sopped around in the gravy after each bite. Then when the dumpling was gone he fished up a chicken leg and ate that, and then a wing, and then the gizzard, and felt better all the time, and pretty soon poured out a cup of coffee and drank that, all before he remembered that he was sick abed and not expected to recover. Then he happened to think, and started back to bed, but on the way there he heard Mr. 'Coon and Mr. Crow talking softly in his room and he forgot again that he was so sick and went up to see about it.

Mr. 'Coon and Mr. Crow had been quite busy up in Mr. 'Possum's room. They had looked at all the things, and Mr. Crow remarked that there seemed to be a good many which Mr. 'Possum had not mentioned, and which they could divide afterward. Then he picked up Mr. Possum's pipe and tried it to see if it would draw well, as he had noticed, he said, that Mr. 'Possum sometimes had trouble with it, and the 'Coon went over to the closet and looked at Mr. 'Possum's Sunday suit, and pretty soon got it out and tried on the coat, which wouldn't need a thing done to it to make it fit exactly. He said he hoped Mr. 'Possum was resting well, after the medicine, which he supposed was something to make him sleep, as he had seemed drowsy so soon after taking it. He said it would be sad, of course, though it might seem almost a blessing, if Mr. 'Possum should pass away in his sleep, without knowing it, and he hoped Mr. 'Possum would rest in peace and not come back to distress people, as one of Mr. 'Coon's own ancestors had done, a good while ago. Mr. 'Coon said his mother used to tell them about it when she wanted to keep them at home nights, though he didn't really believe in such things much, any more, and he didn't think Mr. 'Possum would be apt to do it, anyway, because he was always quite a hand to rest well. Of course, *any one* was likely to *think* of such things, he said, and get a little nervous, especially at a time like this—and just then Mr. 'Coon looked toward the door that led down to the big room, and Mr. Crow he looked toward that door, too, and Mr. 'Coon gave a great jump, and said:

"Oh, my goodness!" and fell back over Mr. 'Possum's trunk.

And Mr. Crow he gave a great jump, too, and said:

"Oh, my gracious!" and fell back over Mr. 'Possum's chair.

For there in the door stood a figure shrouded all in white, all except the head, which was Mr. 'Possum's, though very solemn, its eyes looking straight at Mr. 'Coon, who still had on Mr. 'Possum's coat, though he was doing his best to get it off, and at Mr. Crow, who still had Mr. 'Possum's pipe, though he was trying every way to hide it, and both of them were scrabbling around on the floor and saying, "Oh, Mr. 'Possum, go away— please go away, Mr. 'Possum—we always loved you, Mr. 'Possum—we can prove it."

But Mr. 'Possum looked straight at Mr. 'Coon, and said in a deep voice:

"What were you doing with my Sunday coat on?"

And Mr. 'Coon tried to say something, but only made a few weak noises.

And Mr. 'Possum looked at Mr. Crow and said:

"What were you doing with my pipe?"

And a little sweat broke out on Mr. Crow's bill, and he opened his mouth as if he were going to say something, but couldn't make a sound.

Then Mr. 'Possum said, in a slow voice, so deep that it seemed to come from down in the ground:

"*Give me my things!*"

And Mr. 'Coon and Mr. Crow said, very shaky:

"Oh y-yes, Mr. 'Possum, w-we meant to, a-all the t-time."

And they tried to get up, but were so scared and weak they couldn't, and all at once Mr. 'Possum gave a great big laugh and threw off his sheet and sat down on a stool, and rocked and laughed, and Mr. 'Coon and Mr. Crow realized then that it was Mr. 'Possum himself, and not just his appearance, as they had thought. Then they sat up, and pretty soon began to laugh, too, though not very gaily at first, but feeling more cheerful every minute, because Mr. 'Possum himself seemed to enjoy it so much.

Then Mr. 'Possum told them about everything, and how Mr. Man's medicine must have made him well, for all his pains and sorrows had left him, and he invited them down to help finish up the chicken which had cost him so much suffering.

So then they all went down to the big room and the Crow brought in the big platter of dumplings, and a pan of biscuits and some molasses, and a pot of coffee, and they all sat down and celebrated Mr. 'Possum's recovery. And when they were through, and everything was put away, they smoked, and Mr. 'Possum said he was glad he was there to use his property a little more, and that probably his coat would fit him again now, as his sickness had caused him to lose flesh. He said that Mr. Man's medicine was certainly wonderful; but just then Mr. Rabbit dropped in, and when they told him about it, he said of course the medicine might have had some effect, but that the dumplings and chicken caused the real cure. He said there was an old adage to prove that—one that his thirty-fifth great-grandfather had made for just such a case of this kind. This, Mr. Rabbit said, was the adage:

"If you want to live forever
Stuff a cold and starve a fever."

Mr. 'Possum's trouble had come from catching cold, he said, so the dumplings were probably just what he needed. Then Mr. Owl dropped in to see how his patient was, and when he saw him sitting up, and smoking, and well, he said it was wonderful how his treatment had worked, and the Hollow Tree people didn't tell him any different, for they didn't like to hurt Mr. Owl's feelings.

MR. TURTLE'S FLYING ADVENTURE

MR. TURTLE TELLS ABOUT HIS CHILDHOOD

AND EXPLAINS A VERY OLD FABLE

Once upon a time, when it was early summer in the Big Deep Woods, the Hollow Tree people and Jack Rabbit went over to spend the day with Mr. Turtle, who lives in a very nice stone house which he built himself on the edge of the Wide Blue Water. Mr. Turtle fishes a good deal, and makes most of his living that way, and knows all the best places, so when his friends came he said that perhaps they would enjoy fishing a little— which they could do and sit in a pleasant place at the same time, and talk, and look out over the Wide Blue Water, which was especially blue at this season.

That just suited the Hollow Tree people, for they enjoyed fishing when they had somebody to pick out a good place, and Mr. 'Possum found a nice stump to lean back against, and presently went to sleep, but was waked up soon after, when a big catfish nearly jerked his pole out of his hands. Mr. 'Possum had to use all his strength to pull it out.

Then he was so proud he didn't think about going to sleep again, and told how all his family had been quite smart at catching fish; and pretty soon Jack Rabbit caught a good-sized perch, and Mr. 'Coon hooked a croppie, which got away the first time, though he caught it the next; and Mr. Crow caught a "punkin-seed," which made the others laugh, because it is a funny little fish; while Mr. Turtle just went right along pulling out one kind after another, without saying a word, because fishing is his business and doesn't excite him.

Then by and by the fish stopped biting, as they 'most always do, by spells, and the Deep Woods people leaned back and looked out over the Wide Blue Water, and away out there saw Mr. Eagle swoop down and pick up something which looked at first like a shoe-string; then they saw it wriggle, and knew it was a small water-snake, which was going to be Mr. Eagle's dinner; and they talked about it and wondered how he could enjoy such food.

Mr. Turtle said that Mr. Eagle enjoyed a good many kinds of food, and that he was reminded of an adventure he once had himself with Mr. Eagle, when he (Mr. Turtle, of course) was quite small. Then they all asked Mr. Turtle to tell them his adventure, because they thought it must have been exciting if it was anything like the snake's adventure which they had just witnessed. Mr. Turtle said it was—quite a good deal like it, in some ways—then he said:

"That was the only time I ever flew, or ever had a chance to, or ever wanted to, that I can remember. Very likely you have already heard how once, a long time ago, I thought I could fly, and persuaded an eagle to take me up in the air to give me a start. That old story has been told a good deal, and I believe has even been put into some of Mr. Man's books for his children to read."

Mr. Turtle paused, and the others all said they did remember something of a story of that sort, but never thought it had really happened, because, knowing Mr. Turtle as they did, they didn't believe any of his family would try such an experiment.

"Well," said Mr. Turtle, "it did really happen, though not in the way you have heard. You are right about thinking my family would not care to experiment in that way, and would not do it unless somebody else arranged it for them and gave the experiment a good start."

Mr. Turtle went on to say that in this case it was Mr. Eagle and one of the ancient ancestors of the little water-snake he had just carried off that had started the experiment, though he thought none of it had been really planned.

"I was very small then," Mr. Turtle went on, "about the size of Mr. Man's fist, though I suppose much heavier, for my shell was very thick for my age, and everybody said that if I lived a thousand years or so I might have a shell as big and thick as the one that Father Storm Turtle, up at the Forks, uses to make the thunder with.[1]Then they would laugh and say that Old Man Moccasin, up at the Drifts, would certainly have trouble with his digestion if he ever caught me; which used to scare my mother, for Old Man Moccasin was the biggest water-snake that anybody ever saw, and there was nobody around the Wide Blue Water that didn't give him room, especially fish-fry, and Mr. Frog, and young turtles like me, and even some older ones. My mother used to warn us children all the time, and scold us every day about going away so far from the house and not keeping a good watch-out for Old Man Moccasin, who would surely get us, she said, unless we were more careful. Then she would tell us to look out for Mr. Eagle, too, who was likely any time to come soaring about, and would pick up any food he saw lying handy.

"Well, it used to scare us when we thought about it. Old Man Moccasin was seven feet long, and I judge about a half a foot thick. He could lift himself two feet out of the water when he was swimming, and with his far-sighted glasses on could see a mile. Mr. Eagle was fully twice as big as any of the Eagle family I know of nowadays, and didn't need any glasses to see an article the size of a bug floating on the Wide Blue Water, no matter how high he was flying. We tried to keep a lookout in several directions, but, of course, as we got older without accidents, we grew careless, and our mother used to count us every night and be surprised that we were all there, and give us a good scolding to go to bed on.

"Nothing happened to any of us for a good while, and then it happened to me. I was the biggest and strongest of our lot, and had the thickest shell, and I liked to show how grown-up I was, and would swim out farther, and make believe I wasn't afraid any more of Mr. Eagle and Old Man Moccasin, which wasn't true, of course, for Mr. Eagle could have handled me with one claw and Old Man Moccasin could have swallowed me like a pill and enjoyed the operation.

"Well, one day I was showing off more than usual and had paddled out farther toward the Drifts, saying to the others that I was going to pay a call on Old Man Moccasin. I kept on farther than I intended, for it was a nice summer day and the water felt good. I didn't know how far I had gone until I turned around to look, and then I didn't think about that any more, for a quarter of a mile away, and between me and the shore, was Old Man Moccasin, coming straight in my direction. He was a good two feet out of the water and had on his far-sighted glasses, and I knew he was after me. He was coming, too. He was swimming with a wide, wavy motion, and making a little curl of white foam in front, and leaving a long trail behind.

"I was so scared, at first, that I couldn't do anything. Then I thought I'd better dive, but I knew that Old Man Moccasin could swim faster under the water than on top of it, and see just as well. I began to paddle for dear life toward the other side of the Wide Blue Water, which was a long way off, with Old Man Moccasin gaining fast. I knew he was bound to overtake me before I got across, and I was getting weaker every minute, from being so scared and trying so hard, and I could hear Old Man Moccasin's steady swimming noise coming closer all the time.

"Of course it wasn't very long until I gave up. I was too worn out to swim another stroke. Old Man Moccasin was only about twenty feet away, and when I looked back at him over my shoulder I saw that he was smiling because he was so sure he had me. It was an awful smile, and I don't like to remember it often, even now, and that was ever so long ago, as much as three hundred and fourteen or fifteen years, this spring.

"Well, when I saw Old Man Moccasin at that close distance, and smiling in that glad way, and his spectacles shining, because he was so pleased at the prospect, I said to myself, I'm gone now, for certain, unless something happens right off; though, of course, I didn't see how anything *could* happen, placed as I was. But just as I saidthose words, something did happen—and about the last thing I would have expected. The first I saw was a big shadow, and the first I heard was a kind of swish in the air, and the first I knew I wasn't in the water any more, but was on the way to the sky with Mr. Eagle, who had one great claw around my hind leg and another hooked over my shell, not seeming to mind my weight at all, and paying no attention to Old Man Moccasin, who was beating his tail on the water and calling Mr. Eagle bad names and threatening him with everything he could think of. I didn't know where I was going, and couldn't see that I was much better off than before, but I did enjoy seeing Old Man Moccasin carry on about losing me, and I called a few things to him that didn't make him feel any better.

I said Mr. Eagle and I were good friends, and asked him how he liked the trick we had played on him. I even sang out to him:

"'Old Man Moccasin,
See you by and by;
Mr. Eagle's teaching me
How to learn to fly.'

which was a poem, and about the only one I ever made, but it seemed to just come into my head as we went sailing along. Mr. Eagle, he heard it, too, and said:

"'Look here,' he said, 'what are you talking about? You don't think you could ever learn to fly, I hope?'

"'Why, yes, Mr. Eagle,' I said, 'if I just had somebody like you to give me a few lessons. Of course, nobody could ever fly as well as you can, but I'm sure I could learn to fly some.'

"Then I thanked him for having saved me from Old Man Moccasin, and said how kind he was, and told him how my folks had always told us what a great bird Mr. Eagle was—so strong and grand, and the best flyer in the world—and how we must always admire and respect him and not get in his way, and how I thought if I could only fly a little—perhaps about as much as a hen—I could keep from being caught by Old Man Moccasin, which was the worst thing that could happen, and wouldn't Mr. Eagle please give me a lesson.

"Then Mr. Eagle said, very politely, that he guessed he'd keep me from being caught by Old Man Moccasin, but it wouldn't be by teaching me to fly.

"'You couldn't fly any more than a stone,' he said, 'and a stone can't fly at all.'

"'But a stone can't swim, either, Mr. Eagle,' I said, 'and I can swim fine. I could learn to swim right through the air—I know I could—I can tell by the way I feel,' and I made some big motions with my front legs, and kicked with my free hind leg to show him how I would do it; and I really did feel, the way that air was blowing past, so fresh and strong, that if he would let go of me I could swim in it a little; anyway.

"But Mr. Eagle laughed, and said:

"'You have to have wings to fly with,' he said. 'You couldn't fly a foot. If I should drop you, you'd go down like a shot, and would probably break all to pieces!'

"I was looking down as he spoke, and I noticed that we were passing over Mr. Man's marsh meadows, for we were not flying very high, and I could see locations quite plain, and even some objects. I knew those meadows were soft in places, for I had been there once to a spring overflow picnic. There were also a great number of little hay-piles, which Mr. Man had raked up, getting ready to make his big stacks when the hay was dry. So I said, as quick as I could:

"'Oh, Mr. Eagle, I am certain I could fly this minute. I never felt so much like it in my life. Just give me a big swing, Mr. Eagle, and let me try. If I fall and break, it won't be your fault, and you can take the pieces home to your family. I'll be handier for them that way than any other.'

"When Mr. Eagle heard that, he laughed, and said:

"'Well, that's so, anyway. You people always are a tough proposition for my young folks. Much obliged for the suggestion.'

"And just as he said that, Mr. Eagle quit flying straight ahead and started to circle around, as if he were looking for something, and pretty soon I saw down there a flatstone, and Mr. Eagle saw it, too, and stopped still in the air right over it, as near as he could judge, making all the time a big flapping sound with his wings, until he got me aimed to suit him, and I could feel him beginning to loosen up his hold on my hind leg and shell. Then, all of a sudden, he let me go.

"'Now fly!' he says, and down I went.

"Well, Mr. Eagle certainly told the truth about the way he said I'd drop. I made the biggest kind of swimming motions in the direction of one of those little haycocks, but if I made any headway in that direction I couldn't notice it. I didn't have time, anyway. It seemed to me that I struck bottom almost before I started from the top; still, I must have turned myself over, for I landed on my back, exactly in the center of that flat stone, Mr. Eagle being a center shot.

"He was wrong, though, about me breaking to pieces, and so was the story you've heard. Our family don't break very easy, and as I said before, my shell was thick and tough for my age. It was the stone that broke, and probably saved my life, for if I had hit in a soft place in that marsh meadow I'd have gone down out of sight and never been able to dig out.

"As it was, I bounced some, and landed right side up close to one of those little haycocks, and had just about sense and strength enough left to scrabble under it beforeMr. Eagle came swooping down after me, for he saw what had happened and didn't lose any time.

"But he was too late, for I was under that haycock, and Mr. Eagle had never had much practice in pitching hay. He just clawed at it on different sides and abused me as hard as he could for deceiving him, as he called it, and occasionally I called back to him, and tried to soothe him, and told him I was sorry not to come out and thank him in person, but I was so shaken up by the fall that I must rest and collect myself. Then, by and by he pretended to be very sweet, and said I had done so well the first time, I ought to take another lesson, and if I'd come out we'd try it again.

"But I said I couldn't possibly take another lesson to-day, and for him to come back to-morrow, when I had got over the first one; and then I heard him talking to himself and saying it was growing late, and he must be getting home with something to eat for those brats, and pretty soon I heard his big wing sound; but I didn't come out, for I thought he was most likely just trying to fool me, and was sailing around overhead and waiting, which I still think he was, for a while. After a long time, though,

I worked over where I could see out a little, and then I found it was night, and, of course, Mr. Eagle had really gone home.

"So then I worked along across the meadows, being pretty sore and especially lame in the left hind leg, where Mr. Eagle had gripped me, though I felt better when I got into the Wide Blue Water and was swimming toward home. It took me all night to get there, and the folks were so worried they couldn't sleep, for some one had seen Old Man Moccasin out in the middle of the water, chasing something, during the afternoon.

"Well, of course I told everything that had happened, and almost everybody in the Wide Blue Water came to hear about it, and they told it to others, and Old Man Moccasin heard so much about how Mr. Eagle had fooled him, and how I had fooled Mr. Eagle, that he moved to another drift, farther down, and probably lives there still. And Mr. Eagle heard so much about the way he tried to teach me to fly that he made up a story of his own and flew in all directions, telling it; and that is the story most people know about to-day and the one that Mr. Man put into his books. But it isn't true, and I can prove it."

Mr. Turtle got up and turned around toward the Hollow Tree people. He had his coat off, and he reached back and pointed to a place about in the center of his shell.

"Feel right there," he said, which Mr. Rabbit did, and said:

"Why, there's quite a lump there. It hardly shows, but you can feel it plainly."

"Yes," said Mr. Turtle, "that's where I struck. It was quite sore for a good while. There was a lump there, at first, as big as an egg. It flattened a good deal afterward, but it never quite went away. Feel how smooth it is. It kept just about as it was when it happened."

Then all those other Deep Woods people came up and felt of the queer lump on Mr. Turtle's back, and said how perfectly that proved everything and how Mr. Turtle always could prove things, and they noticed the inscription about the old race with Mr. Hare, and said in some ways Mr. Turtle was about the most wonderful person anywhere and they were certainly proud to be his friend.

Then Mr. Turtle said they might all sit there and talk about it a little, while he went in to cook the fish and make a pan of biscuits and a nice salad for dinner.

THE DEEP WOODS ELOPEMENT

MR. 'POSSUM TELLS ABOUT AUNT

MELISSY AND UNCLE SILAS AND

THE ROMANCE OF MINTY GLENWOOD

One night in the Hollow Tree, when the 'Coon and 'Possum and the Old Black Crow had finished their supper and were sitting around the fire, smoking, Mr. 'Possum said that he thought he had heard Mr. Frog trying off a few notes to-day, over in the Wide Grasslands, so that he knew that it must be coming spring, and Mr. 'Coon said that over Mr. Man's way he had smelled burning leaves, which was a pretty sure sign. Then Mr. Crow said that some of his wild relatives had been cawing about lately, and that was a sign, too. Then they all smoked some more, and looked in the fire, and were glad that winter was about over, and presently Mr. 'Possum said that every time he smelled the spring smell, and heard the spring sounds, it reminded him of something that happened a long time ago, when he was quite young and lived with hisUncle Silas and Aunt Melissy Lovejoy, over beyond the Wide Blue Water. Then the 'Coon and the Old Black Crow begged Mr. 'Possum to tell about it, because they said Mr. 'Possum's stories always sounded so unbelievable, and yet always turned out to be almost founded on fact.

"Well," said Mr. 'Possum, "you remember I told you about Uncle Silas Lovejoy going to the city, once, and coming home all stylish, with a young man to wait on him, and how Aunt Melissy, when she saw them, turned the young man into just a plain hired help and set them both to work in the garden;[2] and you may remember how I once told you about all our folks, including the hired man, being moved by a balloon across the Wide Blue Water and set down right at the very door of a fine hollow tree, which we moved into and enjoyed for a long time—my little cousins and myself growing up there, and some of them still living there to this day."[3]

Mr. 'Possum stopped to fill his pipe again, and the others all said they remembered, and Mr. 'Coon said he always liked the nice slow and reminding way Mr. 'Possum began his stories, as it brought everything up fresh, and one didn't have to be trying to think of what had happened before, but could just sit back and listen. Mr. 'Possum nodded, and lit his pipe, and leaned back and drew a few puffs, as if he enjoyed them so much that he didn't care to go on with his story. But pretty soon he said:

"We lived there till I grew up, and all my little cousins, too, and the hired man stayed with us. He was a very good young man; though, being brought up in town, of course it took him a little while to get used to country ways. But Aunt Melissy was a stirring person and she didn't let it take as long as it might have in another family. Aunt Melissy was quite primpy herself, and said that she guessed she could carry what style there was in our family (being a Glenwood, and having married beneath her), and that Uncle Silas and the rest of us would do pretty well if we managed to keep up with the work she laid out for us; and that was so.

"She kept Uncle Silas and Winters—that was the name of the hired man —busier than anybody, as she never quite got over the trip to town and the way they came home. She used to set Uncle Silas to peeling potatoes, after supper, for next morning, and would make Winters help my young lady cousin do the dishes, which you would not think he would like; but he did. Aunt Melissy didn't know that he would like it so much, or she would have set him at the potatoes, and Uncle Silas at the dishes.

"I don't suppose any of you can guess why our hired man wanted to help my cousin, Minta Glenwood Lovejoy, with the dishes. I couldn't, even after I saw that he was so fond of the job, that he could hardly wait until the supper was cleared away and it was ready for him. I used to wonder how that young man, brought up in town, could take so to such work, and then, after a while, I got to wondering why it took him and Minty Glenwood, as we always called her, so long to get through.

"That was the first thing Aunt Melissy wondered, too. She generally knit a little, after supper, and went to sleep over it, and would wake up suddenly and look at the clock and begin to knit as fast as she could, so we would not think she had been asleep. But one night she slept a long time, and when she looked at the clock it was so late that she said, 'Land's sakes, it's bedtime!' and she went over and shook Uncle Silas, who had gone to sleep with a potato in his hand, and scolded him to bed, and shook up the rest of us, and then noticed that Cousin Minty and Winters were missing, and went straight to the kitchen door and opened it, and found them sitting close together, and Winters holding Cousin Minty's hand and telling her that unless she would set up housekeeping with him he would go back to the city and lead a fearful life; and Cousin Minty Lovejoy looking very scared.

"But she didn't look half as scared as she did when she saw Aunt Melissy, nor the hired man, either. He had to make two trials before he could get up, even after Aunt Melissy told him to, and Cousin Minty Glenwood began to cry, and Aunt Melissy told her to go to bed at once, and made a swing at her, and missed her, as she went by. She didn't miss the hired man, though; and I guess he had something else to think of besides Minty Glenwood and housekeeping, for a few minutes, anyway.

"Then Aunt Melissy Lovejoy told him he could take himself out of that house, and not come back except for meals, and she said he could sleep over in the shop, which was an old, leaky, broken stump of a tree where we kept our garden tools. Then I happened to be sitting in the way, and Aunt Melissy tripped over my feet, and when she righted herself she made a swing at me, too; and if I had not dodged in time I might have been injured for life. As it was, she drove me out with Winters to stay in the shop, and I wasn't sorry, for it was an awful time in our house.

"Next morning, Aunt Melissy Lovejoy was still dangerous, and at breakfast she broke out at things in general, and said the idea that she, a Glenwood, should live to see a hired man sitting up to a child of hers, especially one who was a Glenwood herself, resembling the family as she did, and being named that way, too; which seemed worse, somehow, than anything that ever happened to a Glenwood before, except her own case; and she gave an awful look at Uncle Silas, who got a little spunky —the only time I ever saw him that way—and said he thought that Winters was quite a good fellow and would make as good a husband as *he* had, meaning himself, of course, and Aunt Melissy said, 'Yes, just about,' and asked him if he wanted his daughter to have as hard a row to hoe as *she* had, meaning *herself*, though it was Uncle Silas who had the hard hoeing in that family, if I could judge.

"Well, that night in the shop, Winters and I talked it over, and he decided to go away and take Minty Glenwood with him. He might go to the city, he said, to his folks, who had disowned him because he had been quite wild, but very likely would take him back now that he had reformed and was ready to be tamed by a nice little person like Minty Glenwood. He and Minty would have to elope, of course, and he told me to tell her just what to do, because I could get to see her alone, which he couldn't. There was a little sapling grew near the tree, and one of its limbs stuck out above her window. Winters said he would go out on that limb and bend it down, about midnight, and Minty Glenwood could be there and climb out on it, and they would go away together quite a distance from Aunt Melissy, and live happy ever after.

"So I told Cousin Minty Glenwood about the plan, and just what to do, and she was as scared as a chicken, but said she would do anything to save the hired man from that awful city life he had mentioned. She said she knew something would happen when she tried to climb out her window, but she would have to do it, as it was the only way to get out without going through Aunt Melissy's room, which would be much worse.

"Well, that night Winters and I got everything ready, and had all his things packed in a bundle at the foot of the tree, and a little before midnight by the full moon, Winters went up and crawled out on the limb to bend it down, but when he got there it wouldn't bend far enough to reach Minty Glenwood's window—him being a light-weight person, though I've heard he got fatter later on. He couldn't jump on it, for fear of waking up Aunt Melissy, so he came down and said I would have to go out on the limb, and he would stay on the ground with the things, because I was always pretty solid, even in those days. So then I went out and crawled along on that limb, which bent down with me, all right, but didn't quite reach Minty Glenwood's window, and I couldn't see how she was going to get on it unless she jumped, which I never thought she'd do.

"But you never can tell what a young person in love *will* do. She was there waiting, all dressed in her Sunday things, with a big bundle of what she was going to take along, and when I asked her, in a whisper, if she could jump and grab the limb, she didn't wait to think about it, or to give me notice to get ready, but just jumped, bundle and all, and grabbed the limb with one hand and me with the other, and down we swung, for Minty Glenwood was plump, too, and quite heavy with the bundle, and then she let go and dropped, which I should have done, only I forgot it, and a second later that limb sprung back and sent me sailing up into the sky just about in the direction of the full moon.

"Minty Glenwood landed all right—on her bundle, I heard later—and she and Winters had probably got a good ways on their wedding journey by the time I came down in a brush-heap, where we had been clearing up a new potato-patch. It broke my fall, but it was very stiff, scratchy brush, and when I got out I felt as if I had been in an argument with Mr. Wildcat. I was limping, too, and afraid I was injured internally, for I didn't feel hungry, which is always a bad sign. I was taking on a good deal, and making some noise, I suppose, for when I got to the shop and was going to drag myself up to bed, I heard Aunt Melissy's voice call out the window:

"'What's the matter with you out there? What have you been doing?' And then all at once she gave a howl, for she was in Minty Glenwood's room, and had suddenly discovered that Cousin Minty wasn't in her bed, and hadn't been in it that night. About five seconds later she came tearing out there in the moonlight and grabbed me and says:

"'What does this mean?' she says. 'Where's your Cousin Minty Glenwood and that hired creature, Winters?'

"I could tell from Aunt Melissy's looks and voice that it was not a good time to tell it just as it was. I said I had done all I could to save Minty Glenwood from sorrow, but I had been bruised and scratched in the attempt, and she could see herself that I was bleeding in as many as fifty places and could hardly walk. Very likely, I said, I would not live long enough to tell all the tale, and that I didn't know which way those two fierce young people had gone, which was true enough.

"Then Uncle Silas came out and pretended to be very mad, too, and said it was a shame the way I had been treated. As for Minty Glenwood, she was not worth hunting for, and he would disown her from that moment, though I knew he was as glad as he could be that it had happened, and had a pretty good idea I had something to do with it. Aunt Melissy she stormed and carried on, and said her family was ruined and that she was going back to her folks; but she had gotten more peaceful-like by morning, and put some poultices and bandages on me, and said she didn't see how in time that little, spindly hired man and a mere girl could get a big, strong fellow like me into such a state, though she said, of course Minty was a Glenwood and the Glenwoods were always fighters. Then she took me back to the tree, and gave me Minty Glenwood's room; and when she was out Uncle Silas came to sit with me, and I told him all about it, and he laughed more than I ever saw him laugh at anything, especially when I told about how I went sailing into that brush-heap. Uncle Silas always did like anything funny, and he hadn't many chances to show his taste.

"Well, my appetite came back, but I didn't get well till I had to, because as long as I could be in bed and seem dangerous Uncle Silas had an excuse to sit with me, and we had a fine time. But by and by Aunt Melissy made up some of the worst medicine I ever tasted, which she said she thought would cure me if anything would; which it did, the first dose. Aunt Melissy stayed pretty savage, though, until one day word came from Minty Glenwood, who was now Mrs. Winters, that they were living in town, and that Mr. Winters's people were very fine and stylish and well off, and had taken him back because he had married so well and reformed, and she was as happy as could be. Then you ought to have seen Aunt Melissy show off. Any one would have thought she had made the match, and she couldn't talk enough about Minty Glenwood living in the city, and our fine Winters relatives; and told Uncle Silas he ought to be ashamed of the things he'd said about Minty Glenwood, and ordered him to take them all back, which he did. Then, by and by, she went to visit the Winters folks, and stayed a long time, and Uncle Silas and I and my other cousins had the best time we ever had in our lives. When Aunt Melissy came back she looked as fancy and put on almost as many airs as Uncle Silas had the time he came home and brought the young man who by and by was to marry Minty Glenwood."

Mr. 'Possum sleepily knocked the ashes out of his pipe and yawned and looked into the fire.

"Did you or Uncle Silas ever tell Aunt Melissy about helping Minty Glenwood and Winters to get away?" asked Mr. Crow.

"No," said Mr. 'Possum, drowsily; "we knew Aunt Melissy, and thought it was a pretty good plan to let well enough alone."

COUSIN REDFIELD AND THE MOLASSES

COUSIN REDFIELD BEAR MISBEHAVES

AND IS CURED OF HIS TASTE FOR MOLASSES

The Little Lady has been to the circus during the afternoon and has come home full of it. There were ever so many things to see there, but nicest of all were some little bears—three of them—who rolled over one another in their cage and seemed to be having the best time in the world. She tells the Story Teller all about them after supper; then she says:

"Do you know any story about little bears? Did the Bear family in the Big Deep Woods ever come visiting to the Hollow Tree?"

The Story Teller thinks.

"Yes," he said; "or rather, Mr. Bear came once alone, but that is another story. I know one story, though, about a little bear, a story that Mr. Crow told one night when he had been over to spend the afternoon with Mr. Bear, they being very good friends."

"Mr. Bear told me this afternoon," Mr. Crow said, "about something that happened in his uncle's family some years ago. His uncle's name was Brownwood—Brownwood Bear—and he had a little boy named Redfield, but they called him Reddie, for short. Uncle Brownwood lost his wife one night when she went over to get one of Mr. Man's pigs, and he and little Redfield used to live together in a nice cave over near the Wide Blue Water, not far from the place where Mr. Turtle lives now. Uncle Brownwood used to be gone a good deal to get food and whatever they needed, and Reddie would stay at home and sleep in the cave, or play outside and roll and tumble about in the sun and have a very good time. He had a number of playthings, too, and plenty of nice things to eat, and every morning, before Uncle Brownwood Bear started out he would put out enough to last Cousin Redfield all day—some ripe berries, and apples, with doughnuts, and such things, and always some bread and butter and molasses to finish up on.

"Little Reddie Bear liked all these things very much, but best of all he liked the molasses. Not bread and molasses, but just molasses; and he used to beg Uncle Brownwood to give him a whole saucer of molasses to dip his bread in; but once when his father did that he didn't eat the bread at all, but just ate up the molasses, and was sick that night, though he said it wasn't the molasses that did it, but carrying in some wood and washing the dishes, which he had to do every evening.

"But Uncle Brownwood didn't give Cousin Redfield any more molasses in a saucer; he spread his bread for him every morning, and set the molasses-jug on a high shelf, out of reach, and Reddie used to stand and look at it, when his father was gone, and wonder how long it would be before he would be tall enough to get it down and enjoy himself with the contents.

"One day when Cousin Redfield was looking at the jug he had an idea. Just outside of the cave his father had made a bear-ladder for Reddie to learn to climb on. A bear-ladder is a piece of a tree set up straight in the ground. It has short, broken-off limbs, and little bears like to run up and down on it, and big bears, too, for it gives them exercise and keeps them in practice for climbing real trees.

"When Reddie had the idea, he ran out and looked at his bear-ladder; then he ran back and looked at the jug. If only that bear-ladder was in the cave, he thought, he could walk right up it and get the jug and have the best time in the world. The bear-ladder would go in the cave, for it was a very high cave, and the ladder was not a very tall one.

"But the bear-ladder was fast to the ground, and at first Reddie couldn't budge it. He worked and pushed and tugged, but it would not move. Then he happened to think that perhaps if he climbed up to the top of it, and swung his weight back and forth as hard as he could, he might loosen it that way. So he ran up to the top limbs and caught hold tight, and rocked this way and that with all his might, and pretty soon he felt his bear-ladder begin to rock, too. Then he rocked a good deal harder, and all of a sudden down it went and little Cousin Redfield Bear flew over into a pile of stove-wood, and for ten minutes didn't know whether he was killed or not, he felt so poorly. Then he crawled over to a flat stone and sat down on it, and cried, and felt of himself to see if he was injured anywhere; and he did not feel at all like bothering with his bear-ladder any more, or eating molasses, either.

"But that was quite early in the day, and after Cousin Redfield had sat there awhile he didn't feel so discouraged. His pains nearly all went away, and he began to feel that if he had some molasses now it would cure him. So then he got up and went over to look at the ladder, and took hold of it, and found that it wasn't very heavy, as it was pine, and very dead and dry. He could drag it to the cave easy enough, but when he got it there he couldn't set it up straight. He was too short, and not strong enough, either.

"So little Cousin Redfield went back and sat down on his stone to think again and cry some more, because he found several new hurting places that were not quite cured yet. Then he noticed the clothes-line, and thought he might do something with that. He could get that down easy enough, for it was not very high. Cousin Redfield had often hung out the clothes on it himself. So he untied the ends of the clothes-line and tied one end of it to the top of his bear-ladder, but didn't know what to do with the other end, until he happened to see the big hooks in the top of the cave where his father hung meat when they had a good supply.

"So then Reddie made a bunch of the other end of the rope and threw it at those hooks, and kept on throwing it until after a while it caught on one of them, and enough of it hung down for him to get hold of. Cousin Redfield, for a small bear, was really quite smart to think of all that.

"It wasn't easy, though, even now, to get the bear-ladder up straight. Reddie pulled, and tugged, and propped his feet against the side of the cave, and the table and benches, and got out of breath, and was panting and hot and his sore places hurt him awful, and he thought he'd have to give it up, but at last the end of the bear-ladder caught on the side of the cave where the jug was, and stayed there, and Cousin Redfield could let go of the rope, and get behind the ladder and push, and then, pretty soon, it was up straight, and he could get the molasses-jug as easy as anything.

"It was getting along in the afternoon now, and Reddie knew that Uncle Brownwood Bear was likely to come home before long. So he went right up and got the jug, and nearly dropped it getting down, it was so heavy. But he got down with it all right, and then pulled out the cob that was its stopper, and tipped the jug to pour some of the molasses out in his hand.

"But the jug was quite full, and, the molasses being very thick, would not run out very well. So he tipped the jug over farther, but could only get a little. Then he tipped it on its side, and then pretty soon it commenced to run better, and came out better, and made a nice noise, 'po-lollop, po-lollop, po-lollop,' and formed quite a thick pool right on the floor of the cave, and little Cousin Redfield Bear got down on his hands and knees and licked and lapped, and forgot everything but what a lovely time he was having, and didn't realize that he was getting it all over himself, until he started to get up, and then found it was all around him, and his knees were in it, and everything.

"Cousin Redfield didn't get entirely up. He was nearly up when his foot slipped and he went down flat on his back; when he tried it again he went down in another position, and kept on getting partly up and falling in different ways, until he was an awful sight, and there wasn't so much molasses on the floor any more, because it was nearly all on Cousin Redfield. Then that little bear—little Reddie Bear—suddenly remembered that his father would be coming home presently, and that something ought to be done about it. He was so full of molasses he could hardly move or see out of his eyes. If he could only wipe it off. He had seen his father take a wisp of hay or nice, soft grass to wipe up a little that was sometimes spilled on the table, so Reddie thought hay would be good for his trouble. He would roll in hay, and that would take off the molasses.

"There was a big pile of soft hay-grass in the back part of the cave that Uncle Brownwood used to stuff his mattress with, and Cousin Redfield made for it, and rolled and wallowed in it, thinking, at first, that he was getting off the molasses, but pretty soon finding he was only getting on hay, and really had it all over him so thick that he could not roll any more, and could only see through it a very little. When he managed to get up he had nearly all the hay on him, as well as the molasses.

"Cousin Redfield was really a little walking haystack, and scared at his condition, because he thought he would probably never be a bear any more. He was so scared that he wanted his father to come and do something for him, and started to meet him, as fast as he could, with all that load of hay and molasses. He was crying, too, but nobody could really tell it from the sound he made, which was something like 'Woo—ooo, woo—ooo,' and very mournful.

"Uncle Brownwood Bear was just rounding the big rock there at the turn when he came face to face with Cousin Redfield and his hay. Reddie thought his father would be angry when he saw him, but he wasn't—not at first. Cousin Redfield didn't realize how he looked from the outside, or the lonesomeness of the sound he was making. Uncle Brownwood took just one glance at him, and said '*Woof!*' and broke in the direction of a tree, and of course you could hardly blame him, for he had never seen or heard anything like that before, and it came on him so sudden-like.

"Then poor little Reddie Bear bawled out as loud as he could, 'Pa! Pa! Oh, pa, come back! I's me, pa; come back!'"

"And Uncle Brownwood stopped in his tracks and whirled around and said, in an awful voice, 'You, Redfield!' for he thought Reddie was playing a joke on him, and he was mad clear through.

"Cousin Redfield saw that he was mad by the way he started for him, and became scared, and tried to run away as well as he could; but, not being able to see well, ran right toward the Wide Blue Water, and before he noticed where he was going he stumbled off of a two-foot bank where it was deep, and was down in the water, and had gone under for the second time before his father could lean over and grab him and get him out.

"Poor little Cousin Redfield Bear! By that time most of the hay was washed off of him, but he had got a good deal of the Wide Blue Water inside of him, and was so nearly drowned he couldn't speak. And when his father laid him on the bank, and rolled him, the water and molasses came out, 'po-lollop, po-lollop, po-lollop,' and, feeble as he was, little Cousin Redfield realized that he probably would never care for molasses again.

"When he was empty and could sit up, Uncle Brownwood got a pail, and a dipper, and a brush-broom, and cleaned him on the outside, and then rubbed him dry with an old towel, and put him to bed, though not until after he had scrubbed up the cave so they could live in it.

"Uncle Brownwood Bear did not punish little Cousin Redfield," Mr. Crow said. "He thought Reddie had been punished enough. Besides, Reddie was sick for several days. But Uncle Brownwood put up the bear-ladder much stronger than before, and set the empty molasses-jug in the middle of the table, and kept it there a long time, and when Cousin Redfield tried even to look at it, it gave him such a sick turn that he nearly died."

IN MR. MAN'S CAR

THE HOLLOW TREE PEOPLE HAVE ONE

OF THEIR MOST EXCITING ADVENTURES

Once upon a time Mr. Dog came over to have supper with the Hollow Tree people, and to tell them some news. This, of course, was after he had become good friends with the 'Coon and 'Possum and the Old Black Crow, and enjoyed dropping in for a smoke and a little conversation, especially about Mr. Man's doings, which always interested the Hollow Tree people and their friends.

So on this particular night, when the supper-things had been cleared away, and they all had lit their pipes and Mr. Dog was sitting outside to enjoy the mild evening, he told them something very astonishing. He said he supposed that they had now over at their house (meaning, of course, at Mr. Man's house) the most wonderful thing in the world. He said it was called an automobile, and was a kind of large carriage, but the strange part about it was that it went without any horse or any kind of live thingat all. When Mr. Man brought it home, Mr. Dog said, their Mr. Horse had been looking over the fence into the road, and when he saw that strange object, with Mr. Man sitting in it, holding to a wheel, go flying by, twice as fast as Mr. Horse could run, also making much more noise, and trailing smoke, Mr. Horse gave one snort and took out for the back lots, and they hadn't seen him since. Mr. Dog owned that he himself had thought it best to go under the house, and that he had spent a good deal of the first day there watching Mr. Man open a number of doors and covers that were attached to the new machine, which seemed to be full of sudden noises that Mr. Man could stop whenever he wanted to, though he was not always able to start them with the handle that he turned for that purpose. Sometimes Mr. Man had to turn the handle until he was quite weak before he could get a single noise, and without the noise the carriage would not start.

Mr. Dog said that at first he had been rather uncertain in his feelings toward the automobile, but that, little by little, he had felt more friendly and had come up closer to look at it, only going back under the house again when it started one of those sudden sounds which seemed to make his head ache. Then he got used to those, too, and about the third day Mr. Man suddenly caught him by the collar and invited him to ride, and put him in the back of the carriage, and tied him there with a strong rope so he wouldn't fall out, and so nobody would steal him, because Mr. Man valued him so highly.

Mr. Dog said that when the automobile started he almost wished he *could* fall out, at first, or that somebody would steal him, because he was sure it would effect his heart, and that when they got to going faster and faster he forgot about the rope, and even tried to jump out, but the rope was quite a good one, and probably saved his life. Then pretty soon he didn't want to jump out any more, and laid down on the floor to enjoy it, and was sorry to get home. When Mr. Man was ready to start, next time, Mr. Dog jumped in himself, and the faster they went the better he liked it, and now when they went he often sat up in the front seat by the side of Mr. Man, and if the car was all full of Mr. Man's folks he sometimes sat behind on the top when it was folded back for fine weather. Mr. Dog said there was nothing in the world that he loved so much as to ride in an automobile and to go fast. He said they often went so fast that they passed some of the birds, and that then he would bark loudly to show his enjoyment.

Well, when the Hollow Tree people heard about Mr. Man's automobile they at first could hardly say anything at all. Then Mr. 'Possum said he supposed what made it go was some kind of clockwork that Mr. Man wound up when he turned that crank; and Mr. Crow thought he must build a fire in it to make the smoke come out behind. Mr. Dog didn't know, himself, just how the machinery went in, but that Mr. Man called it a motor and had ever so many names for different parts of it, and sometimes said strong words when he took one of the parts out and couldn't get it back again without trouble. The wheels ran on rubber, he said, rubber filled with air, which Mr. Man pumped into them, and when anything happened to let the air out they had to stop, and then Mr. Man would change the rubber wheel and pump a good deal, and say strong words again, especially when it was warm. Mr. Dog said it was a great comfort to sit back in the shade at such times, and watch Mr. Man pump, and hear him say all the things that he used to say to Mr. Dog himself when he had made some little mistake or had come home later than usual. He said he had never prized anything in his life so much as he had that car, which was what Mr. Man generally called it.

Well, the Hollow Tree people were certainly excited. They said they surely must see that new carriage of Mr. Man's, and if Mr. Dog would send them word some day when he was going out they would hide in the bushes by the road and watch him go by. Mr. Dog said he would do that, and that he and Mr. Man generally took an early ride together, before the rest of the family were stirring, to get some things at the store down at Great Corners—mostly, of late, things for the automobile, which seemed to consume a great deal of smelly liquid, and oils, and all kinds of hardware.

Then Mr. 'Coon said he would give anything in the world to see that automobile going by with the smoke streaming out behind, and Mr. Dog sitting up in the front seat. Mr. Crow said he would give anything in the world to see that, and to slip over to Mr. Man's barn some time when nobody was at home, and really examine the new object, and maybe sit in the seats a little. And Mr. 'Possum said he would give a good deal for all that, but that what he really wanted to do was to sit in the car and ride, like Mr. Dog, as fast as the thing could go.

Then Mr. 'Coon and Mr. Crow both together said, "Oh, we never could do that—never in the world!" and Mr. Dog didn't say anything at all—not at first—but sat thinking. Then by and by he said, all at once:

"I know," he said—"I know a way that you can get to take a ride in our new car.[4] There is quite a big space under the back seat where Mr. Man keeps his pump and sometimes other things, but he keeps most of his things in a tool-box on the side, and only looks into the back-seat place when he needs the pump. When we start out for a long trip he puts Mrs. Man's and Miss Man's extra hats and things in there, but there are none of those articles there now. So if you should come over very early to-morrow morning, before Mr. Man is up, and get into that place under the back seat, you would have just about room enough, and while you couldn't see much, except maybe a little of the road through cracks in the bottom, you would be riding all the time, and always afterward could tell how it felt."

Well, that was such a scary thought that at first the Hollow Tree people couldn't do anything but just sit and shiver and think about how grand and exciting it would be, but how awful if anything should happen. Suppose Mr. Man should have to use his pump, what would be likely to happen then? No one could tell. Mr. Dog said they would have to jump and step lively then, sure enough.

So then they talked about it and gave up the thought, and went on talking about it and giving it up some more, until Mr. 'Possum said that, so far, the worst had never happened to him yet, and that he would take chances if the rest would; and Mr. 'Coon said it would probably be the end of all of them, but he'd risk it; and Mr. Crow said he wouldn't care to pass his life in the Hollow Tree alone, and he might as well go with the others. Then Mr. Dog skipped home as fast as he could go, to listen around and see what Mr. Man's plans were for the next morning, so he would know if they were going on their early trip to Great Corners, as usual, or on some excursion. But he didn't hear anything about a picnic before bedtime, and next morning he was up a little before day, and pretty soon the Hollow Tree people came slipping over, nearly scared to death, and Mr. Dog let them in by his special door to the barn, and they all looked at the automobile, and Mr. 'Possum tried to turn the crank a little, and Mr. 'Coon sat up in the front seat and took hold of the steering-wheel and pretended to be driving, and Mr. Crow said he didn't see how a thing that seemed so cold and dead as that could suddenly come to life and move.

Then Mr. Dog said he heard Mr. Man coming down his back stairs, and they all made a dive for the rear seat, and Mr. Dog put the cushion in place and was outside waiting and barking "Good morning" to Mr. Man when he opened the big barn doors.

Then the Hollow Tree people were nearly dead with scare. Mr. 'Possum whispered that he knew that his heart was beating so loud that Mr. Man could hear it and would think his motor was going, and Mr. 'Coon said if Mr. Man should ever move that back cushion he knew he should die. Mr. Crow said he felt sure this was just some awful nightmare, and that he would wake up pretty soon, and he said of all the dreams he ever had, this was the worst.

But just then Mr. Man got hold of the crank in front of the car and gave it a turn, and then gave it another turn, and then said something, and gave it another turn, and suddenly the Hollow Tree people heard a great number of loud explosions which made them perfectly cold, and then there was just a heavy roar and rumble, and they heard Mr. Man say to Mr. Dog, "Come, get in!" and they felt the automobile begin to move.

That was an awful sensation at first. They could feel that they were going, but the soft rubber wheels did not rattle on the road, and about the only sound was the motor, which they could tell was getting faster and faster as they got out into the smooth road across the Wide Grass Lands, and now and then Mr. Dog barking to them in Hollow Tree language that everything was all right and to rest easy and enjoy themselves—that they were just then passing the Four Oaks, and that presently they would be in the Sugar Hollow Road, and that he wished they could see out and notice how things went spinning by. Then they heard Mr. Man tell Mr. Dog not to make so much noise, and after that things were quieter, and they just heard the steady buzz of the engine, until by and by Mr. Dog barked out that they were at Great Corners and were stopping in front of the store.

The Hollow Tree people whispered to one another that they had certainly enjoyed it, but what a terrible thing it would be if something should happen now, so far away from home, and among so many confusing things. It seemed an age before Mr. Man came back to the car and got ready to start again, and when he did they heard him talking to some other Mr. Man, who asked if he should put the things under the back seat. Then the Hollow Tree people nearly died, until they heard Mr. Man say, "No, never mind, I'm in too much of a hurry to get home; just drop them in behind there, any place," which made them feel a little better, and pretty soon Mr. Man started the motor again, and they felt the car moving faster and faster, the same as before.

The Hollow Tree people couldn't see a thing, but they knew they were riding faster than ever, for they bounced about a good deal, and held on to one another and would have laughed at the fun if they hadn't been too scared. They were pretty anxious for Mr. Man to get the car back into the barn, so they could scamper home as soon as he went in to breakfast, for they had had about all the excitement they wanted. But they got some more in a minute, for all of a sudden, just as Mr. Dog barked to them that they were in the edge of the Big Deep Woods and would be home soon, there came a good deal rougher bumping, and then the car ran slow, and stopped, and they heard Mr. Man say, "A puncture, by gracious! Now I've got to put in a half hour at that pump!"

Those were awful words. He would be back there in a minute, and then what. For a second or two everything was silent, except that they heard Mr. Man getting out of the car, and they got ready to make a wild jump the moment he lifted the seat cover. But then—right at the instant when they expected him to do it—they heard Mr. Dog break right out into a great, big bark, shouting as loud as he could:

"*Come! Come! Come! Mr. Man—it's up a tree!—it's up a tree!—it's up a tree!*" and they knew by the sound that he had jumped out and was calling to Mr. Man to come into the woods near the road, and then, a second later, they heard him call to them, in Hollow Tree words—"Now! now! jump and run! Jump and run! Now! Now! *Now! Now!*"

And the Hollow Tree people didn't have to be told again. All together, they gave a great big push at the cover of the back seat, and lifted it, cushion and all, and scrambled out, and over the side of the car and out the back, and were diving into the deep woods on the other side of the road from Mr. Man, who was looking up a tree and scolding Mr. Dog because he couldn't see anything up there to bark at.

The Hollow Tree people didn't wait to see how it came out, but took out for home, lickety-split, and didn't stop until they were safe in the Hollow Tree. That night Mr. Dog came over to see how they had enjoyed it. He said Mr. Man called him several names because he had not been able to see anything up in the tree, and then had changed the tire and pumped it while Mr. Dog was getting calm. Mr. Man, he said, was surprised to find the back cushion had jumped out of place, but did not suspicion the truth.

Then they all talked it over several times, and were very proud of the great experience, though they decided that they would not try it again.

MR. 'POSSUM'S CAR

MR. 'POSSUM SHOWS HE CAN INVENT

THINGS, ESPECIALLY AN

AUTOMOBILE LIKE MR. MAN'S

"You may remember," said the Story Teller, one evening, to the Little Lady, "my telling you about Mr. Man's automobile, and how the Hollow Tree people, Mr. 'Coon, Mr. 'Possum, and the Old Black Crow, got a ride in it; how Mr. Dog helped them, you know, and just barely managed to keep them all from being caught by Mr. Man."

"Why, yes," said the Little Lady, "and I do hope they never wanted to take another. They didn't, did they?"

Not in Mr. Man's car—no, they had had enough of that, but they were very much excited over it, and thought if they could just sit up in the seat and ride, like Mr. Dog, and see things go by, and not be down under it, in the dark and danger, they would enjoy it more than anything. Mr. 'Possum thought about it, and talked about it, more than anybody, and after breakfast, while Mr. 'Coon and Mr. Crow were doing up the morning's work, he used to walk up and down in the sun and smoke, thinking and thinking, for Mr. 'Possum is quite thoughtful and a good hand to plan, when work doesn't strain his mind.

Well, one morning, when Mr. Crow and Mr. 'Coon were all through, and came out and sat on a log to smoke in the sun and admire Mr. 'Possum, and think how smart he was and how well he looked for his age, he stopped all at once, right in front of them, and said:

"I've got it!" he said. "I can do it! I can make one as easy as anything!"

"Make what?" said the 'Coon and the Old Black Crow, both together, quite excited.

"I can make an automobile," said Mr. 'Possum. "I have planned it all out. I am going to commence now."

Then Mr. 'Coon and Mr. Crow took their pipes out of their mouths and looked at Mr. 'Possum, but couldn't say a word, they were so astonished.

But Mr. 'Possum just threw his head back a little and blew some smoke, and said that it had been quite hard to plan and had taken all of his best thoughts, but that it seemed easy enough now, and that he might have it done by night.

Then the 'Coon and the Crow did get excited, and said: "Oh yes, Mr. 'Possum, we'll help you. Will you let us help you, Mr. 'Possum?"

And Mr. Possum said that of course he would have to do the most, as he would have to show them how, but that they could do all the easy things, and he said they might begin by bringing down the big wood-box out of Mr. Crow's kitchen, and the big wood-saw, and the hammer, and some nails, and any useful tool that they had borrowed from time to time from Mr. Man during his absence.

So then Mr. 'Coon and Mr. Crow ran up and lugged down Mr. Crow's big wood-box, and got the saw and all the other tools and things they could find, and brought them out to a shady place, for it was a fine spring day and getting quite warm, and Mr. 'Possum showed them a round tree, quite large, that had blown down during the winter, and told them they might saw it in two, first, and then cut off four nice slices, two large and two smaller ones, for the four wheels. Mr. 'Possum sat down on the end of the log and showed them just how to take hold of the saw, one at each end, and pull first one way and then the other, and walked around and sighted across it to see that they were keeping it straight, and got a little cooking-grease and put on it, so it would work faster, and Mr. Coon and Mr. Crow worked, and sweat, and tugged, and panted, and said it was wonderful exercise, and by and by really did get the log sawed in two.

Mr. 'Possum said they had done very well for the first cut, which was always the hardest, and that they'd all better rest and smoke a little, as his mind was quite tired with thinking. But in a few minutes he said they might try now to make a wheel, and see if they could do that as well; and Mr. 'Coon and Mr. Crow went at it again, and after a while got a slice of the tree cut off, quite smooth and about an inch thick, and Mr. 'Possum said it would make a very good wheel, but that they would be likely to improve with each slice, and that they must be very careful to hold the saw just as he told them.

So then they rested and cut off another slice, and rested some more, and cut off another slice, until they had four slices, and were nearly ready to drop from being tired and hot, and were saying how fine it was to have that job done, when Mr. 'Possum said that he had just remembered they would need one more slice, for his steering-wheel.

Well, Mr. 'Coon and Mr. Crow thought they would surely die before they got the last slice off, and Mr. 'Possum brought some water and sprinkled a little on their foreheads, and at last that wheel was done, too, and they were all quite exhausted and lay in the shade a while to rest and talk about it. Mr. 'Possum said it might take a little longer than he thought, to finish the automobile, and that it was better not to hurry so, as new thoughts were coming to him all the time. He said that next year they would make another and probably change the style a good deal.

Then when they were rested he showed them some nice straight limbs of the tree that they could saw off for the axles, and when they got those sawed off, which was easier to do, of course, he measured them and showed them how to shave the ends nice and smooth with Mr. Man's drawing-knife, and how to cut out of a strong piece of board some things he called brackets for the back axle to turn in, because the back axle had to turn, and how to bore holes with Mr. Man's auger, in the back wheels and drive them on tight, and how to bore holes in the front wheels and put them on loose with pegs to hold them on, because the front wheels have to turn, and how to bore a hole in the middle of the front axle and in the bottom of the big wood-box, for the steering-rod, because the wood-box was going to be used for the body, and the steering-rod would turn the front axle and hold it to the body at the same time.

Mr. 'Possum said that he had noticed that on Mr. Man's car the steering-rod did not stand straight up, but slanted a good deal, which seemed to him a mistake; no doubt if Mr. Man could see their car he would have his changed. Then the 'Coon and the Old Black Crow said, "Of course," and that there never was anybody so smart to invent things as Mr. 'Possum, and that it was too bad he couldn't go over and suggest thoughts to Mr. Man.

The Hollow Tree people didn't get their car done that first day, but they got it a good deal more than half done, and could hardly wait to get at it next morning. They hurried out right after breakfast, and Mr. 'Possum had Mr. 'Coon and Mr. Crow sawing, and boring, and shaving with Mr. Man's drawing-knife, making the crank, which was a sort of double windlass that stood up in the car over the back axle, built so two people could turn it; and there would be a strong strap that went down through a hole in the bottom of the car and around the axle to make that turn, too, which would drive the car. Then Mr. 'Possum showed them how to make a seat for the front of the box, so he could sit on it and drive and steer, because that was the hardest thing to do, while Mr. Crow and Mr. 'Coon only had to be the motor and work the windlass. Then they got the strap off of Mr. 'Coon's trunk, because it was a very strong one, and put it on, and tightened it up, and Mr. 'Possum said as far as he could see there was nothing more to be done with his car, now, but to use it. Of course he might think of new things later, to attach to it, but he didn't see how he could improve it at present, and that they'd better take it out to the race-track and try it.

So then Mr. 'Possum got up into the seat to steer, and Mr. 'Coon and Mr. Crow pushed, but it went pretty hard, until they put some grease on the wheels and transmission; after that it went better, but squeaked so loud that you could hear it all through the Big Deep Woods, and Mr. Rabbit came kiting over, and Mr. Robin and Mr. Squirrel came skipping among the trees, and Mr. Turtle came waddling up from the Wide Blue Water, to see what new thing was going on over at the Hollow Tree. And when they saw what the Hollow Tree people had made they could hardly speak for their surprise. And when they found out how Mr. 'Possum had done all the hardest part—the planning it and showing how—they said they had never been so proud in their lives, just to be his friend, and they all helped push it over to the race-track, and when they got there Mr. 'Possum invited Mr. Rabbit to sit in the front seat beside him, because Mr. Rabbit was an author and would want to write something about it; and Mr. Robin and Mr. Squirrel and Mr. Turtle went down the track a piece to see them dash by.

Then Mr. Crow and Mr. 'Coon took hold of the windlass, and Mr. 'Possum told them not to start too suddenly or go too fast at first, as it might injure the transmission, which was quite delicate. So Mr. 'Coon and Mr. Crow put a little strength on the windlass, but it didn't turn. Then they put some more on it, but it didn't turn. Then they put all they had on it and it turned just a little bit, but very slow. Mr. 'Possum said he didn't think it would be dangerous to go a little faster, and Mr. Coon and Mr. Crow turned with every bit of strength they had, and worked harder even than they had at sawing up the log, but still Mr. 'Possum said he didn't believe they were going quite as fast as Mr. Man's car had travelled, and Mr. Turtle called to them that perhaps if he and the others pushed until they got it to going well, and the machinery warmed up, it might run better.

Mr. 'Possum didn't much like to have his car pushed, but he said that Mr. Man's car didn't always start well, either, and very likely had to be pushed sometimes. So then Mr. Turtle and Mr. Squirrel got one on each corner, and Mr. Robin went ahead to kick stones out of the road, and Mr. 'Possum said "Ready!" and everybody did his best, and the Deep Woods automobile squeaked and squealed and started down the race-track pretty fast, but not always keeping in the middle of it, because Mr. 'Possum couldn't steer perfectly the first time, and went from one side of the road to the other, and said it was because they didn't push evenly, and he was as proud as could be of his great invention. Then Mr. Squirrel and Mr. Turtle gave it one big push, and let go, and Mr. 'Coon and Mr. Crow ground away at the windlass their level best, and the car went on quite a ways before it stopped. It wouldn't have stopped then if Mr. Coon and Mr. Crow hadn't given clean out and let go of the crank and hung over the sides of the car and said it was all so exciting and they were enjoying it so much that they were quite overcome.

Then Mr. Turtle said *he* had an idea. He said down not far from his house which stood by the Wide Blue Water there was a smooth road with a good deal of a slant in it, and that if the car was over there and got started down that slant it would very likely almost run itself and move a good deal faster. So they all said yes, that was just the thing, and everybody but Mr. 'Possum took hold and pushed, because Mr. 'Possum had to steer; and by and by they got to the slanting road, which was, really quite a hill, and Mr. Rabbit got in again by Mr. 'Possum, and Mr. 'Coon and Mr. Crow took hold of the windlass, and sure enough, that time, the car started well enough, and went without any trouble at all. Mr. Turtle and the others had run a good ways down the road to see them pass, and pretty soon they did pass, going faster and faster every minute, and everybody cheered and waved, and Mr. 'Possum called back to Mr. 'Coon and Mr. Crow that they could turn a little slower, so all could enjoy the scenery.

But Mr. 'Coon and Mr. Crow *couldn't* turn any slower, and when they tried to hold back on the crank it just jerked them right around, and when they let go entirely they went even faster, for that slanting road had turned into a real hill, and they were going down it as speedy as Mr. Man would go down, and perhaps speedier, and Mr. 'Possum wasn't looking at the scenery any more, but was holding as fast as he could to the steering-wheel, trying to keep in the road, and not doing it the best in the world, though nobody was pushing now.

Then all at once Mr. 'Possum saw something that scared him—scared him so he nearly fainted away, for just then they rounded a turn, going lickety-split, and right in front of him Mr. 'Possum saw the Wide Blue Water. They were headed straight for it, and Mr. 'Possum's thoughts became confused. He could only realize two things clearly—one was that he had forgotten all about putting brakes on his car, to stop with, and the other was that he *must* stop without delay, or they would all disappear in the Wide Blue Water, and that he couldn't swim.

Mr. 'Possum wondered very rapidly what would stop them, and just then he saw a little tree ahead, right at the side of the road, and he thought *that* would probably do it. He couldn't think of anything *but* that, and he steered for the tree as straight as he could, which wasn't so very straight, for he hit it on the bias.

Still, that was enough to stop the car, but not the people in it. Mr. 'Possum himself flew into a thick blackberry-patch and lost consciousness; Mr. Rabbit sailed clear over the blackberry-patch, and landed in a boggy place, which was soft enough, but quite splashy; Mr. 'Coon went straight up into the little tree they had hit, and grabbed some limbs and hung on, while Mr. Crow just opened his wings, though he hadn't used them for ever so long, and went sailing over to a nice grassy place by the road, and wasn't injured at all.

There wasn't really anything fatally damaged except the automobile. When Mr. 'Possum came to, and Mr. Rabbit cleaned some of the bog off of himself, and Mr. Crow came back, and Mr. 'Coon climbed down, and the others caught up with them, they all looked around to see what they could find of Mr. 'Possum's invention. Some of it was in the bushes and some in the tree, and two of the wheels they couldn't find at all. Mr. 'Coon said his trunk-strap was as good as ever, which was more than Mr. Crow could say for his wood-box. Mr. 'Possum, who limped and seemed suffering, said, when he looked at what they had gathered, that he felt just about as his car looked—a good deal broken up and hardly worth carrying home. Then he said that very likely Mr. Man had had the same experience with his first car, and that next year's model would be different in several ways.

Then Mr. Turtle took Mr. 'Possum on his back, and everybody said it was very fine for the first time, and certainly most exciting, and the Hollow Tree people invited all the others to the Hollow Tree to celebrate Mr. 'Possum's great invention. They stayed quite late, and when Mr. Rabbit started home he said he would certainly write a poem on all the events.

MR. BEAR'S EARLY SPRING CALL

AN UNWELCOME VISITOR PAYS

A VISIT TO THE HOLLOW TREE

Once upon a time when it had been a hard winter in the Big Deep Woods, and spring was late, and there was still very little in the way of fresh food to be had, Mr. 'Possum came in quite excited, one evening, and after bolting the down-stairs door put a heavy prop against it, though he called up first to see if Mr. 'Coon and Mr. Crow were both in.

"*I'm* in," Mr. 'Coon called back. "I hunted till I was tired and couldn't find a thing worth bringing home, except some winter parsnips that I dug out of Mr. Man's garden."

"*I'm* in," Mr. Crow called back. "I found a beefsteak that Mr. Man had hung out to freeze. I'll cook it with Mr. 'Coon's parsnips. Why, is anything the matter?"

Mr. 'Possum came puffing up the stairs to the big room, and sat down before the fire, and took off his shoes and warmed himself a little, and lit his pipe, and said:

"Well, there *may* be, if we don't keep that prop pretty firmly against the down-stairs door. I met Mr. Robin while I was out, and he tells me that a new Mr. Bear has moved over into the edge of the Big Deep Woods, into that vacant cave down there by the lower drift. His name is Savage—Aspetuck Savage—one of those Sinking Swamp Savages, and he's hungry and pretty fierce. They've had a harder winter in the Swamp than we have had up here, and when Aspetuck came out of his winter nap last week and couldn't find anything, he started up this way. Mr. Man has shut up all his pigs, and Mr. Robin thinks that Aspetuck is headed now for the Hollow Tree. Somebody told him, Mr. Robin said, that we manage to live well and generally come through the winter in pretty fair order, though I can tell by the way my clothes hang on me that I've lost several pounds since Mr. Man built that new wire-protected pen for his chickens."

Mr. 'Coon said the news certainly was not very good, and that while his condition was not so bad for such a hard season, he didn't propose to let Mr. Aspetuck Savage use him in the place of pork, if he could help it. Mr. Crow said he didn't feel so much afraid on his own account, as Aspetuck would not be apt to have much taste for one of his family, unless his appetite was extremely fierce, though, of course, it was safer to take no chances. So then they all went down-stairs and put still another prop against the door, and piled a number of things behind it, too, to make it safe. Then they went up and Mr. Crow cooked the nice steak and put some fried parsnips with it, and Mr. 'Possum said if it wasn't for thinking of Aspetuck he could eat twice as much and get his lost weight back; and Mr. 'Coon and Mr. Crow told him he had better keep right on thinking of Aspetuck, so there would be enough to go around. By and by they all sat before the fire and smoked, and got sleepy, and Mr. 'Coon and Mr. 'Possum went up to their rooms to bed, but Mr. Crow said he would nap in his chair, so that if Mr. Savage Bear should arrive early he would be up to receive him.

"Tell him I'm very sick," said Mr. 'Coon, "and too run down and feeble to get up to make him welcome."

"Tell him I'm dead," said Mr. 'Possum. "Say I died last week, and you're only waiting for the ground to thaw to bury me. Tell Aspetuck I starved to death."

Mr. Crow said he would tell as many things as he could think of, and then he sat down by the fire, and did not really intend to go sound asleep, but he did, and the fire went down, and Mr. Crow got pretty cold, though he didn't know it until all of a sudden, just about sunrise, there was a big pounding knock at the down-stairs door, and a big, deep voice called out:

"Hello! Hello! Wake up! Here's a visitor to the Hollow Tree!"

Then Mr. Crow jumped straight up, and almost cracked, his joints were so stiff and cold, and Mr. 'Coon heard it, and jumped straight up, too, in his bed; and Mr. 'Possum heard it, and jumped straight up in *his* bed, and Mr. 'Coon said, "'Sh!" and Mr. 'Possum said, "'Sh!" and Mr. Crow stumbled over to the window and opened it and looked out, and said: "Who's there?" Though he really didn't have to ask, because he knew, and besides, he could see the biggest Mr. Bear he ever saw, for Aspetuck Savage was seven feet tall, and of very heavy build.

"It's me," said Mr. Bear, "Mr. Aspetuck S. Bear, come to make a spring morning call." You see, he left out his middle name, and only gave the initial, because he knew his full name wasn't popular in the Deep Woods.

"Why, Mr. Bear, good morning!" said Mr. Crow. "How early you are! I didn't know it was spring, and I didn't know it was morning. I'm sorry not to invite you in, but we've had a hard time lately, and haven't cleaned house yet, and I'd be ashamed to let you see how we look."

"Oh, never mind that," said Mr. Aspetuck Bear. "I don't care how things look. I forget everything else in the spring feeling. I only want to enjoy your society, especially Mr. 'Coon's. I've heard he's so fine and fat and good-natured, in his old age."

When Mr. 'Coon heard that he fell back in bed and covered his head and groaned, but not loud enough for Aspetuck to hear him.

And Mr. Crow said: "Ah, poor Mr. 'Coon! You have not heard the latest. The hard winter has been a great strain on him and lately he has been very poorly. He is quite frail and feeble, and begs to be excused."

"Is that so?" said Mr. Bear. "Why, I heard as I came along that Mr. 'Coon was out yesterday and was never looking better."

"All a mistake—all a mistake, Mr. Bear. Must have been his cousin from Rocky Hollow. They look very much alike. I'm greatly worried about Mr. Coon."

"Oh, well," said Mr. Savage Bear, "It doesn't matter much. Mr. 'Possum will do just as well. So fine and fat, I am told—I was quite reminded of one of Mr. Man's pigs I once enjoyed."

When Mr. 'Possum heard that he fainted dead away, but was not so far gone that he couldn't hear what Mr. Crow said. Mr. Crow wiped his eyes with a new handkerchief before he said anything.

"Oh, Mr. Bear," he called back, "it's so sad about Mr. 'Possum. We shall never see his like again. He had such a grand figure, and such a good appetite—and to think it should prove his worst enemy."

"Why—what's the matter—what's happened? You don't mean to say—"

"Yes, that's it—the appetite was too strong for him—it carried him off. Mr. 'Coon and I did our best to supply it. That is what put Mr. 'Coon to bed and I am just a shadow of my old self. We worked to save our dear Mr. 'Possum. We hunted nights and we hunted days, to keep him in chicken-pie with dumplings and gravy, but that beautiful appetite of his seemed to grow and grow until we couldn't keep up with it, this hard year, and one day our noble friend said:

"'Don't try any more—the more I eat, the more I want—good-by.'"

Mr. Crow wiped his eyes again, while Mr. Bear grumbled to himself something about a nice state of affairs; but pretty soon he seemed to listen, for Mr. 'Possum was smacking his lips, thinking of those chicken pies Mr. Crow had described, and Mr. Bear has very quick ears.

"Mr. Crow," he said, "do you think Mr. 'Possum is really as dead as he might be?"

"Oh yes, Mr. Bear—at least twice as dead, from the looks of him" (for Mr. 'Possum had suddenly fainted again). "We're just waiting for the ground to thaw to have the funeral."

"Well, Mr. Crow, I think I'll just come up and take a look at the remains, and visit *you* a little, and maybe say a word to poor Mr. 'Coon."

When Mr. 'Coon and Mr. 'Possum heard that they climbed out of their beds and got under them, for they didn't know what might happen next.

And they heard Mr. Crow say: "I'm awfully sorry, Mr. Bear, but the down-stairs door is locked, and bolted, and barred, and propped, and all our things piled against it, for winter; and I can't get it open until Mr. 'Coon gets strong enough to help me."

"Oh, never mind that," said A. Savage Bear, "I can make a run or two against it, and it will come down all right. I weigh seven hundred pounds."

Mr. 'Coon and Mr. 'Possum had crept out to listen, but when they heard that they dodged back under their beds again, and got in the darkest corners, and began to groan, and just then Mr. Bear gave a run and flung himself against the down-stairs door with a great bang, and both of them howled, because they couldn't help it, they were so scared, and Mr. Crow was worried, because he knew that about the second charge, or the third, that door would be apt to give way, and then things in the Hollow Tree would become very mixed, and even dangerous.

Mr. Crow didn't know what to do next. He saw Mr. Savage Bear back off a good deal further than he had the first time, and come for the downstairs door as hard as he could tear, and when he struck it that time, the whole Hollow Tree shook, and Mr. 'Coon and Mr. 'Possum howled so loud that Mr. Crow was sure Mr. Bear could hear them. They were all in an awful fix, Mr. Crow thought, and was just going to look for a safe place for himself when who should come skipping through the tree-tops but Mr. Robin. Mr. Robin, though quite small, is not afraid of any Mr. Bear, because he is good friends with everybody. He saw right away how things were at the Hollow Tree—in fact, he had hurried over, thinking there might be trouble there.

"Oh, Tucky," he called—Tucky being Mr. Aspetuck Savage Bear's pet name—"I've brought you some good news—some of the very best kind of news."

Mr. Bear was just that minute getting fixed for his third run. "What is it?" he said, holding himself back.

"I found a big honey-tree, yesterday evening," Mr. Robin said. "The biggest one I ever saw. I'll show you the way, if you care for honey."

Now Mr. Bear likes honey better than anything in the world, and when he heard about the big tree Mr. Robin had found he licked out his tongue and smacked his lips.

"Of *course* I like honey," he said, "especially for dessert. I'll be ready to go with you in a few minutes."

Mr. 'Coon and Mr. 'Possum, who had crept out to listen, fell over at those words, and rolled back under the beds again.

"But you ought not to wait a minute, Tucky dear," Mr. Robin said. "It's going to be warm when the sun gets out, and those bees will be lively and pretty fierce."

Mr. Savage Bear scratched his head, and his tongue hung out, thinking of the nice honey he might lose.

"It's beautiful honey, Tucky—clover honey, white and fresh."

A. Savage Bear's tongue hung out farther, and seemed fairly to drip. "Where is that tree?" he said.

"In the edge of the Sinking Swamps," said Mr. Robin. "Not far from your home. You can eat all you want and carry at least a bushel to your folks. You ought to be starting, as I say, before it warms up. Besides, a good many are out looking for honey-trees, just now."

Mr. Aspetuck Savage Bear just wheeled in his tracks and started south, which was the direction of the Sinking Swamps.

"You lead the way," he called to Mr. Robin, "and I'll be there by breakfast-time. I'm mighty glad you happened along, for there looks to be a poor chance for supplies around here. I've heard a lot about the Big Deep Woods, but give me the Sinking Swamps, every time." Then he looked back and called "Good-by, Mr. Crow. Best wishes to poor Mr. 'Coon, and I hope Mr. 'Possum's funeral will be a success."

And Mr. Crow called good-by, and motioned to Mr. 'Coon and Mr. 'Possum, who had crept out again a little, and they slipped over to the window and peeked out, and saw Mr. Aspetuck Savage Bear following Mr. Robin back to the Sinking Swamps, to the honey-tree which Mr. Robin had really found there, for Mr. Robin is a good bird, and never deceives anybody.

HOW MR. 'POSSUM'S TAIL BECAME BARE

MR. 'POSSUM RELATES SOME

VERY CURIOUS FAMILY HISTORY

Once upon a time, when it was a very pleasant afternoon, and the Hollow Tree people were sitting along the edge of the world, hanging their feet over and thinking, Mr. 'Possum went to sleep, and would have nodded himself off into the Deep Nowhere if his strong, smooth tail hadn't been quite firmly hooked around a little bush just behind him. All the others noticed it, and said how lucky it was that a person of Mr. 'Possum's habits had a nice, useful tail like that, which allowed him to sleep in a position that for some was thought dangerous even to be awake in. Then they wondered how it happened that Mr. 'Possum's family had been gifted in that peculiar way, and by and by, when he woke up, and stretched, and moved back in the shade, and leaned against a stump to smoke, they asked him.

Mr. 'Possum said it was a very old story, because it had happened about a hundred and fifty-six great-grandfathers back. He had heard it when he was quite small, he said, and would have to think some, to get it straight. So then he shut his eyes and smoked very slowly, and about the time the Deep Woods people thought he was going to sleep again he began telling.

"My family is a very ancient one," he said—"one of the oldest in the Big Deep Woods, and there used to be only a few, even of us. That was when Mr. Painter, or Panther, as we say now, was King of the Deep Woods, and he was very fond of our family, which helped to make them scarce, and was one reason why they got to slipping out at night for food, when Mr. Painter was asleep.

"We were a pretty poor lot in those days, and whenever Mr. Painter took after one of my ancestors that ancestor would make for a tree and run out on a limb that was too small to bear up Mr. Painter, and just cling there, because Mr. Painter would climb up, too, and shake the limb, and very often he would shake an ancestor down, like a papaw, and the only thing to do then was to make for another tree, or if the next tree was too far, to play dead, because Mr. Painter did not much like anything he hadn't killed himself. That is how we got the playing-dead habit, which others sometimes try and call it 'playing 'possum,' because nobody can do it so well as our family, and I judge some of our family didn't do it perfectly the one and only chance they got to try it, or else Mr. Painter was smarter, or hungrier, at those times.

"Well, my ancestors got so that they could hold to those limbs very firmly with their hands and feet, and Mr. Painter had a hard time to shake them down, though he didn't like to give up, and would go on shaking all day, sometimes, until my folks would get tired out. They used to try to hold and brace themselves with their tails, too, but we had just big, ornamental tails in those days, covered with thick, bushy hair, and of very little use, like Mr. Squirrel's and Mr. 'Coon's."

When Mr. 'Possum made that remark, Mr. 'Coon and Mr. Squirrel sat up quite straight, and were just about to say something, but Mr. Rabbit motioned to them and said "'Sh!" and Mr. 'Possum went right on, without noticing that anything had happened.

"Those tails were no manner of account, but just in the way, and some of my folks thought it would be almost better if they didn't have them at all, but just a funny bunch of cotton, or something, like Mr. Rabbit's."

When Mr. 'Possum said that, Mr. Rabbit sat up quite straight, and was just about to say something, but Mr. 'Coon and Mr. Squirrel motioned to him and said "'Sh!" and Mr. 'Possum didn't notice anything had happened.

"You see," he went right on, "every little while it happened that one of my ancestors would start up the tree not quite soon enough, and Mr. Painter would just manage to get his claws in that bushy ornament, which would settle it for that ancestor, right away. Of course, my family were proud of those big, plumy things, people being generally proud of their most useless property, something they would be better off, and live longer, without. My folks thought those great tails were handsome, especially our young people, who would walk about waving them and practise carrying them in new positions, and about once a week would do up the long, thick fur on them in little knots, tied with tough, twisted grass, which would make the hair curl and look very showy indeed. Even some of my ancestors who happened to get old acted in that foolish way, and when the fur got thin would wear some kind of false stuff, though any one but a blind person could always tell it.

"Well, one day a new and very handsome Mr. 'Possum came into the neighborhood, from some place nobody had ever heard of before, and none of our folks had ever seen anything like him. He was stouter than our breed and lighter colored, and had a very long, bushy tail that curved in a peculiar way and stayed beautifully curled, without ever being put up in grass at all. He said so, and my ancestors watched him, to prove it.

"That young man called himself Somers, and he certainly became popular with the young Miss 'Possums of our section. They went crazy over him, and of course that made all the young Mr. 'Possums jealous of him, though they would have given anything to be like him. They knew they couldn't be that, so they hoped something would happen to him, and used to tell him of nice new an interesting walks to take when they thought Mr. Painter might be in that neighborhood. Then they would follow, and hide around in the bushes and watch, expecting some time to see Mr. Painter get his claws into that curly blond duster before Somers could reach a limb, or shake him down afterward.

"Well, just as they expected, one day when Somers went out for a little promenade alone Mr. Painter happened along, but Somers saw him first, and made for a tree, with Mr. Painter after him, reaching for that fine plume and just missing it, as the handsome stranger went up the tree and out on a limb, with Mr. Painter right behind and making very savage noises. Then he began shaking the limb as hard as he could, and my ancestors, who were watching from quite a safe place, thought Somers would drop pretty soon, for they didn't think he could be trained to holding on—such a fine person as he was.

"So they watched, very hopeful, and sure enough, about the third hard shake Somers dropped—just let go with his hands and feet, and rolled off, almost as if he really didn't care. My ancestors said that was what it looked like, and that was what it was. Somers didn't care at all, for when he let go and dropped, he didn't fall, but just swung off into space, and stayed attached to that limb, hanging head down, by his tail!

"My ancestors had never been so astonished in their lives, nor Mr. Painter, either. He couldn't believe it. He thought at first Somers had got caught, somehow, and gave one more shake, but when Somers swung back and forth, laughing and calling out, 'Much obliged, Mr. Painter— much obliged for the nice swing!' Mr. Painter climbed down and took out for home as hard as he could, without looking behind him, for he thought it was some kind of magic. And pretty soon Somers climbed down, too, and brushed himself off a little, and fixed his tail in a nice position, and walked along, smiling; and my ancestors hurried to him and said they had just arrived in time to witness his great performance, and begged him to show them how he did it, and offered him anything if he would only teach them to handle those useless ornaments of theirs in that grand way.

"So then Somers told them all about it. He said he was the inventor of the idea, and of the medicine that made it work. He said he was very soon going back to his own people, but before he went he would make up some medicine, which would make their hair and tails both curl, and would explain how to take it.

"Well, they were so anxious about it that he began next morning, and sent out different ones for different things—special kinds of roots, and several sorts of very twisty things, such as grape-vine clingers, and honeysuckle, and a great lot of love-vine—that yellow stuff that winds about everything and can choke even a ragweed to death. Then he put it all into a big kettle, and had them pour water on it and put a fire under it, and he boiled it for two days and nights, without letting the fire get down, and after that poured it off into a big gourd to settle, and told them just what size swallow to take of it, and how to practise the new habit when they felt the curling begin. Then he said he must be going, as his family would be worried about him being away so long, and my folks all gathered to see him off, and gave him as many presents as he could carry, and he went away somewhere to the southeast, and they never saw him again.

"Of course, as soon as he was gone, and the medicine was settled nice and clear, our whole family collected to take it. There wasn't a 'possum in the Deep Woods that wasn't there, and they had to get in line, because every one wanted to be first and be sure to get some of that magic juice.

"Well, perhaps they were too anxious, and took bigger swallows than Somers told them to, or it may be the stuff was a little too strong, or Somers got in too much of the love-vine, which has such an awful twist; or it may be he wanted to play a joke on some of our family for being jealous and wanting to get him caught by Mr. Painter—whatever it was, that medicine had an awful power and did even more than he said it would. When every one had taken a good swallow, except the last one in line—he being a middle-aged person named Waters, who had to take what was left, which was only about a spoonful and very disappointing to Mr. Waters—they all felt the curling sensation begin, and commenced the new muscle-practice Somers had mentioned; and just then Mr. Painter, who had probably heard that Somers had gone, came tearing through the timber, and my folks quit practising, and broke for trees and limbs, with Mr. Painter after one plump young chap which he didn't quite get, and pretty soon was shaking a limb in the usual way, only harder, being hungrier than common. The plump young person was scared half to death, never having had much practice holding on, anyway, and in about a minute he was obliged to let go with his hands and feet, and just give up everything, shut his eyes, and drop, expecting next minute he would hit the ground and it would be all over.

"But right there that plump young fellow got the best surprise of his life. He had been so scared that he had forgotten all about Mr. Somers's medicine, but the medicine hadn't forgotten about him. During the little minute he had been sitting on that limb his tail had curled itself around it as tight as if it had grown there. Mr. Painter couldn't have shaken him loose in a week. He hung down just like Somers, only not so far, and he didn't swing much, because that strong medicine had taken up all his slack and there was very little room for play. He didn't care for that, of course, not then. He got brave and very cheerful right off, and called out to Mr. Painter, just like Somers:

"'Much obliged, Mr. Painter—much obliged for the nice swing. Swing me again, Mr. Painter.'

"And when the rest of our folks saw that the same thing had happened to all of them they all let go and dropped, and began calling from the different trees: 'Come and swing us, too, Mr. Painter—stay all day and swing the rest of us!'

"And when Mr. Painter heard that, and looked around and saw all my ancestors hanging head down and making fun of him, he thought the whole Deep Woods was full of the strange magic, and he piled down out of that tree and took out for the bushes, and was never seen in the Big Deep Woods again.

"My folks called after him just as far as they could see him, and when they were sure he was gone they thought they would come down and celebrate. But they didn't do it—not just yet. There wasn't one of them that could unwind himself from his limb, except old Mr. Waters, who had got only a teaspoonful of the medicine, which very likely was just about the right amount. Mr. Waters swung quite loose and free from his limb, and got down without much trouble, and it took him all the afternoon to go around from tree to tree and pry the rest of my ancestors loose, and unwind them, because those new-fangled tails would snap together like springs, and it took several days' steady practice and straightening before they were really useful at a moment's notice. By that time, another strange thing had happened: The fur on them had curled so tight at first that it was like very close wool; then it kept right on getting tighter and tighter until it seemed to curl itself clear out, and by the end of the week there wasn't one of our family whose tail wasn't as bare as your hand, except old Mr. Waters, who had a handsome curly plume, like Somers's, and became a great curiosity, the only one that we ever had like that in our tribe.

"All the others thought the fur would grow again, but it never did, and when they got used to its absence they decided they were much better off without it, especially since they had learned the Somers habit, which they said worked easier and better in the new, smooth form. They were sorry, at first, that Mr. Somers had not left them the recipe for that medicine, on account of the new little 'Possums that would be coming along. But they didn't need the recipe. That medicine was strong enough, the amount they took, to do our family at least a thousand generations, and maybe more. Somers never came back, and they never heard of him again. Some of my ancestors used to say that he was not a real person at all, but something that could take different shapes and work magic, just as Mr. Painter believed he did. Anyhow, he was a great blessing to our family, as you may have noticed."

Mr. 'Possum moved over to the Edge of the World in the sun, hooked his tail about the same little bush, and went to sleep again. The other Deep Woods people looked at the way he did it, as if it was something new that they had never seen before.

Mr. 'Coon said: "I think I'd like a little, just a little, of that medicine; Mr. 'Possum's gift certainly would come handy at times."

Mr. Squirrel nodded.

Mr. Rabbit looked out over the Deep Nowhere, and said nothing at all.

A DEEP WOODS WAR

MR. 'COON TELLS A CURIOUS

STORY OF LOVE AND BATTLE

Once upon a time Mr. Dog came over to the Hollow Tree to spend the evening with the 'Coon and 'Possum and the Old Black Crow, and pretty soon other Deep Woods people dropped in, and everybody was passing the time of day and feeling comfortable and happy in the good society of those present. They talked about the weather, and how it seemed to be a dry spring, and Mr. Rabbit said his garden was suffering, and Mr. Turtle said he had never seen the Wide Blue Water so low at this season for a hundred and nine or ten years. He couldn't remember just which it was, but it was the year that Father Storm Turtle, who lives up in the Big West Hills, and makes the thunder, was laid up with misery in his shoulder, and Mother Storm had to run the thunder-works, and tend to sick folks, too. Most people, Mr. Turtle said, believed that good, loud thunder helps to shake the rain out of the clouds, and very likely it was so, for the next spring, when Father Storm got well, he gave them enough of it, and it rained so that the Wide Blue Water came up into the Big Deep Woods as far as the Hollow Tree, which wasn't a Hollow Tree then, but a good, sound oak only about four hundred years old,—his Uncle Tom Turtle, who lived up by the Forks, having been just about that old himself when it came up as a sapling.[5]

When Mr. Turtle got through, none of the Hollow Tree people said anything at all, at first, for whenever Mr. Turtle mentioned how old he was, and the great ages of many of his family, it seemed to them too wonderful for words. But by and by Mr. Dog said that Mr. Turtle was very likely right about the thunder making the rain, for he had heard Mr. Man explain that the reason it was so dry this year was because there was a great war going on, on the other side of the world, with big guns roaring all day and night, and that the terrible jar and noise of those guns kept it raining there steadily, so there was no rain left for this side. Mr. Dog supposed that Father Storm Turtle could not get up a noise big enough to beat that war noise, and had about given up trying.

Then Mr. Rabbit asked why Mr. Man's people wanted to have war and fire those big guns at each other, which must be very dangerous and very apt to kill people, besides causing floods in one place and drought in another, which was bad for everybody concerned.

Mr. Dog said Mr. Man himself didn't know why all those Mr. Man's over there wanted to have a war. Mr. Dog had heard Mr. Man say that those people over there didn't know themselves what it was all about, and that they were killing each other every day by the thousand with those big guns, and losing all their property, for no reason at all that anybody could think of, except, perhaps, to take each other's country, which probably wouldn't be worth much now, whoever got it. Mr. Dog said that, of course, Mr. Man's people were very smart in many ways, but that as nearly as he could find out they had always been very silly about wars, and had fought many of them, for no good reason, instead of being wise like the Deep Woods people, who only fight to get something to eat, or sometimes when there are rivals at a time of courtship. Mr. Dog said his own people were more like Mr. Man's, probably from association, and that more than once at Great Corners he had been set upon by a perfectly strange Mr. Dog, without cause; but even then it was generally a single-handed affair and soon over, except once, when he believed every Mr. Dog in Great Corners took a hand for a few minutes, though nobody was hurt and everybody seemed to feel better for the exercise.

Mr. Dog went on to say that he seldom enjoyed these occasions, and lately had stayed in Mr. Man's car while they were at Great Corners and talked earnestly to any strange dog that came around looking for war.

Then Mr. 'Coon, who hadn't said a word so far, but had just been smoking and thinking, seemed to wake up out of deep reflection, and said:

"I know something about war. I thought of making one, once, and afterwards I saw one."

Then everybody looked at Mr. 'Coon, who is usually rather quiet, and asked him to please tell about those wars—nothing could be more interesting, just now, than to hear about them.

So Mr. 'Coon filled his pipe up fresh, and told them.

"Well," he said, "there isn't much to tell about the first one. I was quite young, and there was a family lived not far from us who had a young Miss 'Coon that I thought I would like to set up housekeeping with, and when I mentioned it she was a good deal in the notion, too. Everything seemed to be going along quite well until, one day, another young Mr. 'Coon came along and saw Violet—that was her name—and he had the same plan that I had. He belonged to that family over near the Jagged

Bluffs—a common, oversized lot, with no style to speak of. I had never seen him, myself, when I first heard about his coming to call on her, and made up my mind I would fight him the first time we met. Then I thought I had better get a look at him and study his weak points, without him seeing me; so I hid in the bushes one afternoon, near Violet's house, to watch him pass. When, pretty soon, he came along and I saw the curious shape and size of him, I decided that Violet was not worthy of me. He was very wide forward, and his hind legs were set in a peculiar way. I can't imagine what Violet could see in him."

Mr. 'Coon sighed and took time to fill his pipe before he went on.

"That was the war I thought of making," he went on, after a minute or two, "and that was all there was of it. I took a walk over to see a good friend of mine, in those days, a young Mr. Bear named Redfield, generally called Cousin Redfield, or Reddie. Mr. Crow once told us about some of his little-boy adventures, as you may remember. Well, I found Cousin Redfield and told him what had happened, and he said he would go with me and help me fight that spread-shouldered ruffian, and asked me what were his weak points. I said I hadn't noticed any, and we decided that we wouldn't bother with him, and went to visit a honey-tree that Cousin Redfield had found and thought of robbing, some night. I said I didn't think it was right to rob the bees of their honey, but that we would go and look at it, to take my mind from less pleasant things.

"So we walked a good ways until we came to it, and it was there that I saw the other war that I mentioned. It seems there were several swarms of bees in that tree, itbeing quite a big one with a number of hollow limbs. Every year when the young bees had made new swarms they had moved into vacant limbs, until, I suppose, the tree had become quite full and pretty crowded. I don't know what had started the trouble, but there was a good deal of it going on when we got there. Perhaps some strong new or old swarm was trying to drive out a weak one and take its place. Anyway, there were about a million of those bees buzzing and whirling about outside, and you could smell that they were mad, and you could see that they were fighting, for there were dead ones on the ground, and they were pattering down on the leaves quite fast. Cousin Redfield and I first thought it was sprinkling, until we saw that the falling drops were dead bees.

"But that was nothing to what happened a few minutes later. For all those other swarms, one after another, pretty soon began to pour out from the different holes in the limbs and body of the tree, and join in the war, until the air around that tree was just black with fighting bees, and the dead ones were coming down so thick that I would not have cared to stand under it without Mr. Man's umbrella.

"Cousin Redfield and I got off a little ways to watch it. Cousin Redfield said that perhaps we ought to interfere, but I said that it wasn't our war, and that it would be better to wait and see what we could do when it was over.

"So we got in a good safe place and looked on, and I never thought anything could be like it. I don't know how those bees could decide which side they were on, or what they were fighting about, or which side was which. They must have been all relatives once, and would be all cousins, or something, now. They all looked exactly alike to Cousin Redfield and me, and pretty soon they got very thick on the ground, like a kind of black moss or something, that was spreading and piling up deeper every minute and doing nobody any good, and not deciding anything, that we could see. Cousin Redfield and I made up our minds that they had all gone crazy.

"I don't know how many millions of those bees there were, but they made a noise like Mr. Man's automobile when it is running at high speed, and that mad-bee smell was so strong that it seemed to Cousin Redfield and me almost dangerous to stay there. So we got a little farther away, for we didn't know but that all those bees might suddenly decide to quit fighting one another, and make a rush at us. But that didn't happen. They were too busy with their war. They kept on pouring out of the tree until there were no more left to come, and that black cloud whizzed and stung and smelled, and the black moss on the ground kept growing and spreading until we could see that the live ones were thinning out. By and by there were more bees on the ground than there were in the air, and we thought they would quit then and go to work, but they kept right on until they were more than shoe-top deep on the ground and just about ordinarily thick in the air, and still fighting.

"I don't know how long it was that Cousin Redfield and I stood there watching those bees kill one another, but I know by sunset there were not more than a dozen or two left, and they were roosting about on the limbs and leaves, worn out or crippled, and not able to fight any more.

"Then Cousin Redfield said he thought it was time for us to interfere and see what could be done, so we each broke off a little birch brush and swept a path through that black bee moss, and looked into the hole at the bottom of the tree, but couldn't hear anything. So we climbed up a little ways and pretty soon came to honey—bushels of it. There were no bees there except a few fat, lazy ones that couldn't sting, and were probably kings or queens or something, and we didn't mind them. We ate all the honey we could, and went home, and next morning got baskets and all day long carried honey out of the bee-tree and had enough to last our families for a whole year, the best honey I ever saw in the Big Deep Woods, and the *most* I ever expect to see.

"We didn't get it quite all, though, for the second morning when we came back we found the tree occupied. Violet and that big, rough creature from the Jagged Bluffs had found it, and started housekeeping there, with enough honey to last them at least a month. I heard later they called it their honeymoon, and I believe people sometimes call the first few weeks of being married by that name still.

"Cousin Redfield said he would help me drive them out, if I said so; but I said no, that place had seen war enough, and with all the honey we had at home I could get along without the present contents of the tree, so we went away. I said that something would probably happen to those two for the way they had done, and I was right. For about six weeks later the honey smell of that tree brought another big, new, strong swarm of bees to settle there, and they turned Violet and her thick-necked partner out, in about two minutes, and took full possession. Cousin Redfield Bear and I used to walk over that way every day, to observe things, and we happened along just as it was going on. That fellow's wide build didn't help him any against bees. Violet came out first, pawing her nose with one hand, and knocking bees with the other. He stayed to fight a little, but directly he rolled out, scratching and pawing, and five minutes later his own mother wouldn't have known him, he was so swelled. Violet looked at him, and then at me and Cousin Redfield laughing at him, and I think would have deserted him for me, then; but Violet herself had one eye closed, and her nose was the shape and size of a reversed turnip. I saw then that I had never truly loved her and had been wise to give her up. They left the country soon afterwards and I don't know what became of them. That honey-tree blew down one winter night about a year after, and then Cousin Redfield and I went back and got some more honey, but not as much as we did after the great war."

The Hollow Tree people hadn't said a word during Mr. 'Coon's story, but when he had finished Mr. Dog said so far as he could see there was just about as much sense in that war as there was in the one going on over on the other side of the world, and that the war over there would very likely end in about the same way.

But Mr. 'Possum said that Mr. 'Coon's war was a good deal better than Mr. Man's, because, being so soon over, nothing but those silly fighting bees was wasted; and for Mr. 'Coon and Cousin Redfield Bear to have stayed out of it until there was no more fighting, and then go in and carry off a wagon-load of honey, was probably the smartest thing they had ever done in their lives.

MR. CROW AND THE WHITEWASH

I

THE OLD BLACK CROW TRIES

A STRANGE EXPERIMENT

One very nice May morning when Mr. Crow went over to call on Jack Rabbit, he found him whitewashing his back fence, and after Mr. Rabbit had showed Mr. Crow how fine it looked when it was dry, he took him into the kitchen, which he had whitewashed the day before, and Mr. Crow went on about it and said it was the nicest thing he ever saw, and if he just knew how, and had the things to do it with, he would whitewash his own kitchen in the Hollow Tree.

Then Mr. Jack Rabbit said it was the easiest thing in the world—that all one needed was a little quick-lime and some water and a brush, and then some practice in putting it on so it would look nice and even, and not spotty and streaky, as was so liable to be the case when one had not learned how. Mr. Rabbit said he had borrowed some quick-lime early one morning from Mr. Man's lime-kiln, over in the edge of the Big West Hills, and that Mr. Crow could get some at the same place if he went early enough and took a basket to bring it home in. Jack Rabbit said that you must put the lime into a barrel, or a tub, or something, and then pour water on it, which would make it hot and smoky, quite suddenly, which he supposed was the reason it was called quick-lime, but that by and by it would grow cool and turn white, when it was called "slack" lime, and then it only needed some more water to make the beautiful, clean whitewash which Mr. Crow admired so much. As for practice, he said, he would let Mr. Crow try a little on his back fence.

So then Mr. Crow and Jack Rabbit went back to the fence job, and Mr. Rabbit stirred the whitewash and dipped in the brush, and made a few strokes, right and left, and then crossed them up and down, and then right and left again, to get the material on nice and smooth, and stood off to look at it until it began to look white and clean, because the sun was hot and dried it very fast; and pretty soon he let Mr. Crow have the brush.

Mr. Crow did very well for the first time, and kept improving right along, and Jack Rabbit sat in the shade, where it was cool, and let Mr. Crow go on practising and improving, until he had whitewashed almost all the fence, and felt so hot and warm he was about ready to drop, beside being dazzled from looking at the boards that got as white as snow, with the hot sun shining on them.

Then all at once Mr. Crow noticed something else. He had not been very careful about splashing the whitewash and had got some of it on different parts of himself, and especially on the wing that he worked with, and when he stopped and looked at it, he said, "Good gracious!" for wherever the whitewash had got on him he was not black any more, but snow white.

And right then Mr. Crow had an idea. He put the brush in the pail, and came over and stood in front of Jack Rabbit, and said:

"Why can't you whitewash me?" he said. "I've always thought it would be pleasant to be white, for a change. I heard of a white crow, once, in our family, and I always wondered how he got that way. Of course he must have been whitewashed—I can see it, now, as plain as anything. I am sure you could whitewash me, Mr. Rabbit, with all the practise you've had, so that none of the black would show. Whitewash me for Sunday, Mr. Rabbit, and I will go home and give Mr. 'Coon and Mr. 'Possum a great surprise."

Well, Mr. Rabbit was delighted. He dearly loved to try experiments, and prepare surprises, and to show how well he could do things. He said he believed he had heard of people being whitewashed for Sunday, and that Mr. Crow, who was so nice and smooth outside, would be just the one to be fixed up in that way. He said Mr. Crow might need more than one coat to make him seem perfect, but that he would take time and do a good job. Then he said he had a smaller brush in the house, for fine work, and would get it right away.

Mr. Crow was already in hot weather costume and only had to lay off his vest for Jack Rabbit to begin, and pretty soon Mr. Rabbit came back with the fine brush and went to work. He told Mr. Crow to shut his eyes and keep them shut until the stuff was dry, as it might smart a little if it ran in them, and to stand in the sun, which Mr. Crow did. Jack Rabbit began at the top and whitewashed clear down to his feet, and then told him to turn around slowly, so the sun could get on all sides of him, and get him dry enough for a second coat.

So Mr. Crow turned around and around, and kept his eyes shut, and got quite dizzy, before Mr. Rabbit told him he could open his eyes now and see how he liked his appearance as far as gone. And Mr. Crow looked and said he liked it very much, though he was pretty streaky in places. Mr. Rabbit said the next coat would surprise him, and told him to shut his eyes again, which Mr. Crow did, and Jack Rabbit gave him another and very heavy coat, from head to foot. Then when Mr. Crow had turned and turned in the sun to dry himself, he looked again and was quite pleased. He was almost entirely white, now, and Mr. Rabbit said one more coat would fix him.

So then Mr. Rabbit gave him the last coat and laid the whitewash on thicker than ever, especially in places, and when Mr. Crow could open his eyes he went in and looked at himself in Mr. Rabbit's long glass, and said he never thought anything so astonishing as that could happen to anybody, and declared he must hurry right off home now, and that he was going to make up a lot of whitewash and keep himself looking like that all the time, and his kitchen, too, and perhaps all the rest of the Hollow Tree, for there was certainly nothing in the world so wonderful as whitewash.

Then Mr. Crow thanked Mr. Rabbit and hurried off, but pretty soon walked slower, for, as he got dryer and dryer, the thick whitewash got stiffer and more caky, and Mr. Crow cracked a good deal as he walked, and he was afraid his nice new color might come off if he wasn't careful.

Mr. 'Possum and Mr. 'Coon were taking a nap in the sun when Mr. Crow got back to the Hollow Tree, and didn't hear him until he was standing right in front of them. Then they both woke up at once and took one look at the strange, white creature standing over them, almost blinding in the sun, and each one thought at first he was having a very wonderful dream, and couldn't speak for enjoying it. But when Mr. Crow started to come closer they were not so sure about the dream, and both gave a big jump and made for the down-stairs door of the Hollow Tree, and got inside and bolted it tight.

That, of course, made Mr. Crow laugh, but not loud enough for them to hear him, and pretty soon he went to the door and tried the latch, and then knocked, and Mr. 'Possum called out—

"W-wh-who's there?"

"Why, it's me!" said Mr. Crow. "What have you got the door bolted for?"

And Mr. 'Coon called out, "Oh, Mr. Crow, did you see anything out there?"

"Why, no," said Mr. Crow. "What made you think so."

And Mr. 'Possum said, "W-we saw something very strange out there, Mr. Crow—a v-very curious bird!"

"I guess you were dreaming," said Mr. Crow. "There is no bird out here but me, that I know of. Open the door so I can come in and get the dinner."

So then Mr. 'Possum and Mr. 'Coon pulled back the bolt and opened the door, but when they saw Mr. Crow standing there, so white and shining, Mr. 'Possum fainted and Mr. 'Coon got behind a barrel until they heard Mr. Crow laugh and ask them if his new complexion had changed him so they didn't know him?

Then Mr. 'Possum came to, and Mr. 'Coon came out, and Mr. Crow told them all about how it happened, and they all went out in the sun again, and Mr. 'Coon and Mr. 'Possum walked around Mr. Crow and admired him and talked about his great change, and Mr. 'Possum touched him and said his complexion seemed pretty solid, somewhat like a shell, and Mr. Crow told him how he had to move rather carefully in it, at first, though very likely it would limber up in time. Then he told them how he was going to do the kitchen that way, and perhaps other things, and they all got excited and talked about it, and Mr. 'Possum said that probably he would have them give him a coat next winter, to match the snow which would be handy, nights when he was borrowing chickens from Mr. Man, though he supposed he would have to be dipped. Then they went in to dinner, and Mr. Crow set out such things as did not require much exercise, and by and by they all talked about it a great deal more and decided to have a regular cleaning up and whitewashing, like Mr. Rabbit's. Mr. 'Coon said he and Mr. 'Possum would do the cleaning up if Mr. Crow would attend to the whitewashing, as he had learned how, and they would all begin next day.

II

WHAT CAME OF MR. CROW'S

GREAT EXPERIMENT

Well, Mr. Crow slept sitting up in a chair that night, for fear of damaging his new complexion, and next morning was out very early with a basket, on the way to Mr. Man's lime-kiln in the edge of the Big West Hills.

It had rained a little in the night, and Mr. Crow was rather afraid he might get his new complexion wet on the bushes, so he stepped very carefully and was not really comfortable, though proud of his looks. He was gone a good while, but Mr. 'Coon and Mr. 'Possum were still asleep when he got back, so he emptied his lime into an old barrel behind the stove where he intended to mix it by and by, and started the breakfast before calling them. They didn't get up right away, though, so Mr. Crow sat down and had a cup of coffee and a biscuit or two, and then called to them that he was going over to borrow Mr. Rabbit's whitewash brush. He might be a little while getting back, he said, but that they could start their job any time.

So then he left, and Mr. 'Coon and Mr. 'Possum had their breakfast, and talked about what they would do, and decided that Mr. 'Coon could set things to rights in the house, and Mr. 'Possum could rake the leaves. After that they had some more coffee and talked some more, and Mr.

'Possum stretched and said he hadn't slept very well, and didn't know as he cared so much about cleaning up things this morning as he had yesterday, but he supposed they must be getting at it, as Mr. Crow seemed to have his mind set on changing things in general since Mr. Rabbit had got him started in the direction of whitewash, which improved him, of course, in some ways; though it certainly made him less homelike and familiar and seemed to affect his cooking.

Then Mr. 'Possum yawned again and went down-stairs and got the rake, and went out and began to make a few little piles of leaves, which were quite wet from the rain, and did not rake very easy, and made him tired. So pretty soon he called up to Mr. 'Coon, who was sweeping and moving furniture, and asked him what he should do with the leaves, as they were too wet to burn, and if he left them there until they were dry the wind would blow them all about again.

Mr. 'Coon looked out the up-stairs window and told him he'd better fetch them up and put them in something in Mr. Crow's kitchen, so he could have them to light his fire with when they got dry. Then pretty soon he came down and helped Mr. 'Possum, and they carried them up, and saw Mr. Crow's barrel, and threw them in until it was quite full, then poked them down and put in some more, and said how glad Mr. Crow would be to have them, and that now they would go outside and rest a little, until they saw him coming.

So they went out and sat on a log and smoked, and were wondering what kept Mr. Crow so long, when Mr. 'Possum said he smelled something curious, and just then Mr. 'Coon happened to look up at the window, and said:

"Goodness gracious alive, if the Hollow Tree isn't on fire!"

Then Mr. 'Possum looked up, too, and said, "As sure as you're born, and we shall lose everything!"

And just then they saw Mr. Crow coming, on the run, for he had seen it even before they had—Mr. Crow being always a great hand to see things.

"Hurry up, and get out our things," he said; and didn't stop, but ran right to the door and up the stairs, with Mr. 'Coon and Mr. 'Possum after him, though there was a good deal of smelly smoke there, and they expected the flames to break out any minute. Mr. Crow said the fire seemed to be in the kitchen, and commenced to grab the parlor furniture and hand it to them, and Mr. 'Possum called to him to get his best suit out of his room, if possible, as he never expected to be able to afford another. Mr. 'Coon ran through to his room, and brought out some pictures he thought a good deal of, and came dragging his trunk with his free hand, and slipped when he got it to the stairs, and rode down on it like a sled, while everybody worked carrying and throwing things, and Mr. Crow forgot all about his fine new complexion, which began to crack off and scatter until it was all over the floor and stairs. Then pretty soon they all felt so choky from that queer smelly smoke that they went out in the air and piled up their things at a safe distance and stood, waiting for the flames to break out and burn down their big Hollow Tree they had lived in so long.

But for some reason the flames did not break out, and by and by the smoke seemed to get less. Then it really got a good deal less, until there wasn't any to speak of, and after a while the Hollow Tree people went to the down-stairs door and looked in, and, though there was plenty of smell, there was no smoke. Mr. 'Possum said it smelt a good deal like Mr. Man's lime-kiln on a wet morning. Then Mr. Crow had an idea.

"Did you put anything in that barrel behind the stove," he said to Mr. 'Possum and Mr. 'Coon.

"Why, yes," Mr. 'Coon said, "we put in the leaves that Mr. 'Possum raked up. They were wet, and we put them there to dry, so you could have them to cook with."

Then Mr. Crow went straight up the stairs and back to his kitchen, and there was the barrel of leaves, still smoking a little, though not much, for the lime was about "slacked." Mr. Crow took hold of the barrel, and Mr. 'Coon and Mr. 'Possum, too, and they carried it down-stairs and outside, and when they got it far enough away from the tree they emptied it out and kicked the leaves over the lime, which was still smoking a little and seemed very hot. Then Mr. Crow looked down at himself, and said:

"I don't care much about whitewash, anyway."

And Mr. 'Coon and Mr. 'Possum looked at him, too, which they had been too busy to do before, and Mr. 'Coon said:

"It doesn't seem to last very well."

And Mr. 'Possum said, "Mr. Crow, you have a new complexion every day."

For the whitewash had come off of Mr. Crow in patches, until he looked like a black-and-white crazy quilt. And just then it began to rain again, and they all hurried to carry in their things; and when they got them all in the tree again Mr. 'Coon and Mr. 'Possum began to straighten them, but Mr. Crow said he thought he would go outside a little and enjoy the shower. Then pretty soon it poured pitchforks, but still Mr. Crow didn't come in, and when Mr. 'Coon and Mr. 'Possum looked out of the upper window they saw him hopping about in it, and waving, and sometimes rolling in the leaves, and mopping his face as if he liked it better than anything; and by and by, when the rain was over and he came in, there was no more whitewash, and he was the blackest, shiniest Old Black Crow that ever was.

Then Mr. 'Coon said that, after all, there was nothing like a natural complexion.

And Mr. Crow said: "The trouble about whitewash is that it's too hard to keep it on."

Mr. 'Possum, who was resting in a big chair, after his hard morning's work, opened his eyes just long enough to say, "It's too hard to live up to"; and went sound asleep.

MR. 'COON'S STAR STORY

MR. 'COON EXPLAINS THE STARS

AND HOW THEY ARE MADE

One very pleasant June night the Hollow Tree people and Jack Rabbit walked over to the edge of the world and sat down to talk and smoke and look at the stars.

Mr. 'Possum said he always liked to look at the stars when he had anything on his mind, because they seemed so far away from all his troubles, and if he looked at them long enough his troubles seemed to get far away, too. He said he supposed the stars were fully two miles away, some of them, though the little ones would have to be closer or one would not be able to see them. Very likely the moon, being so big, might be farther away than any, and if it was really another world, as Mr. Rabbit had once explained to them,[6] it must be still a good deal bigger than it looks, and very far away, indeed, probably as much as seven miles, though no one would think so to see it coming up full on a clear night behind the Blackberry-patch. Mr. 'Possum said that once, when he was quite young, he had tried to get over there to catch it, but had not been able to arrive in time.

Then all the Hollow Tree people and Jack Rabbit looked up at the sky— at the different kinds of stars, and the patterns they made, such as the Big Dipper, and the Seven Sisters, and at the Milky Way, that seemed broader and milkier than usual; and nobody said anything, until Mr. 'Coon happened to remark:

"I saw Mr. Man *making* the stars, once. It was very interesting, though dangerous; I nearly got hit by one."

Then Mr. Rabbit and the others were very much interested, and Mr. Rabbit said:

"What a curious idea! How is it you never told us about that before?"

"Well," said Mr. 'Coon, "it was a good while ago, and the only people I told about it then didn't believe it. I haven't thought of it for a long time, and, besides, I supposed all smart people knew about Mr. Man having that job, and the careless way he works at it."

"I wish you would tell us," said Mr. Rabbit, "if you can remember clearly just what you think happened on the night you speak of."

"I don't think anything about it," said Mr. 'Coon. "It was a good while ago, but I remember exactly how it was as well as if it were only last week. I'm not likely ever to forget it. It was this way:

"We needed a chicken pretty badly in our family, and my big brother, who generally went after them, said it was about time I was learning to do something, and sent me over to Mr. Man's to get it. I was very young, and nobody had ever told me the best way to go about borrowing a chicken from Mr. Man. Chickens used to roost in trees near Mr. Man's house, in those days, and I knew my folks generally waited until he had gone to bed, which I supposed was only because they didn't like to disturb him. It is too bad that grown people do not explain things carefully to young folks—it would save many accidents.

"Well, I liked the idea of being sent for a chicken. It made me feel grown up. I didn't care to be out late, though, so I started quite early—about sunset—and walked along slowly, enjoying the evening, for it was summer-time, early in July—the Fourth—a date I am sure I shall never forget.

"It was a good ways from our place to Mr. Man's house, and it was about eight o'clock when I got there. Mr. Man and his folks had not gone to bed yet, but were out in the yard doing something, or getting ready to do something, and I was very much interested to know what it was. I really forgot all about the chicken I had come for, and went up quite near and sat in some young gooseberry-bushes to watch things.

"Mr. Man and Mrs. Man and their little boy all seemed to be very busy. They brought some chairs out in the yard, and a table with a pitcher and some glasses—in case they were thirsty, Mrs. Man said, it being so warm

—and then Mr. Man brought out a box of things, and Mrs. Man told him to set it some distance off, to avoid accidents, so he set it just over by the gooseberry-bushes, quite close to me. I didn't know what Mrs. Man meant then by avoiding accidents, but I did later.

"I wanted ever so much to see what was in that box, and decided that presently, when they got interested in something else, I would step out and take a look at it. But they seemed to be interested in the *box* most of the time, and Mr. Man's little boy kept asking every minute if it wasn't dark enough now, and by and by Mr. Man said he thought it was, and came over to the box and took out something and carried it over where the others were, and seemed to be striking a match, and then, all at once, there was a great swishing sound, and a long tail of fire that went climbing to the sky, and when it got there suddenly seemed to blow up and send out six or seven of the most beautiful stars, while Mr. Man's little boy jumped about and shouted, 'Hurrah for the Fourth of July!' Being pretty badly scared, I didn't see just what became of those stars, but I suppose some of them are among those we see up there now, though perhaps some of them didn't stick, but turned into falling stars, then, or later on.

"Well, Mr. Man and his little boy kept right at work making the stars, as hard as they could, and I had a very good time, while it lasted. I came out of the gooseberry-bushes where I could see well, and every time they sent up a batch of stars on that tail of fire and Mr. Man's boy shouted and danced, I danced about, too, and felt like shouting for the Fourth of July, which I decided must be star-making day every year.

"But most of all I was anxious to see in that box. It seemed quite dark inside, and I couldn't understand where all the fire that they made the stars out of could come from, and I don't understand that part of it yet. I only know what happened next, which was this:

"Mr. Man and his little boy seemed to get through with the first part of the star-making performance, for I heard Mr. Man say, 'That's all of those. Now we'll have the Roman candles,' which I judged must be some different stars, perhaps little ones, because Mr. Man's boy said, 'Oh, I can do those—I can do the Roman candles.' Then Mr. Man came over and got something out of the box again, and I couldn't stand it any longer, I was so curious; so when he had gone back I slipped over and peeked in.

"It was light enough for my eyes, and I could make out a number of curious-shaped little packages still in the box—some round and long, some round and short, and some flat like wheels or six-cornered, and some coiled around and around like little snails, and nothing among them like anything I had ever seen before. I couldn't imagine how those things could make stars, and was just about to take out one and examine it when there was a bright light and the Roman candles began to work and send up beautiful round stars right above our heads, first one way and then another, lighting up everything quite plainly. Just then Mr. Man's little boy must have looked in my direction, for he shouted right out, 'Oh, look! there's a young coon!' and, without stopping to think, being so young himself, he aimed his Roman candle in my direction, and shot those stars straight at me. One big yellow one just grazed my left ear and scared me so I couldn't move at first. Then a big red one singed my back fur, and I commenced to dodge and get in motion. And just then a big blue star-ball came straight toward me. I thought I was gone then, but I wasn't. It didn't hit me; it fell short and went in the box.

"Well, there must have been ever so many of the best stars wasted that night. Before I could get fairly turned around those curious things I had seen in there began to go off. You never heard such a popping and fizzing and spluttering and banging, and you never could imagine such a flashing and flaming and wriggling of dangerous materials as that blue star-ball started.

"Of course I didn't stay right there to enjoy it. About the first pop that came from that star-box I was headed in the other direction and up a tree, where I could get a good view and be out of range. It was most exciting. Every minute something new came out of that box—fiery snake things, and whirlers, and all sorts of fancy stuff, and things like bouquets of flowers, which I suppose would have been up there in the sky now for us to look at, if they hadn't been wasted so recklessly; and Mr. Man and his family all came running with pails of water, but were afraid to get near enough to put it on, until the star-stuff was nearly used up; and just then I noticed a scared chicken on the limb next mine, so I took it and went home, though it wasn't a very good one, being picked out in that careless way.

"I told my folks about seeing Mr. Man and *his* folks making the stars, but they didn't think much of my story. When I showed them the singed place on my back they said that I had probably been shot at, as I deserved to be for trying to borrow a chicken before Mr. Man had gone to bed, and that I had imagined or made up the rest. But I hadn't, for it all happened just as I have been telling it now. I don't know whether Mr. Man makes stars on the Fourth of July every year or not. I could have gone back to see if I had wanted to, but I didn't want to. I saw him do it once, which was plenty; and if he hadn't wasted a lot of his stuff we would have some finer stars than any I can see up there now."

Mr. Rabbit smoked thoughtfully a minute. Then he said: "That is certainly a very remarkable story, but I can't believe that those were real stars that Mr. Man and his family were making. I think those must all have been just shooting stars, and meteors, and comets and such things, that are always flying about and changing. There is a story in my family that accounts for the other stars, and seems more probable, because it happened a very long time ago, when 'most anything could be true and when all the first things began."

"Very likely," said the 'Coon, "but what I saw was plenty true enough to suit me, while it lasted."

MR. RABBIT'S STAR STORY

JACK RABBIT TELLS OF HIS GRANDPAW'S

LONG LADDER THAT TOUCHED THE SKY

This is the story that Jack Rabbit told to the Hollow Tree people when they sat together on the edge of the world, and hung their feet over the Big Nowhere and looked at the stars.

"Well," he said, "you may remember my telling you once about the moon being a world, and how, a long time ago, my folks used to live there, and all slid off one day, when the moon tipped up on its edge, and they were not holding on."

Mr. 'Possum said that he remembered quite well, and that Mr. Rabbit's story had seemed to explain everything—at the time. Of course, he said, an explanation couldn't be expected to last forever, and if Mr. Rabbit would like to make a new one, that would be even better, they would be glad to hear it, because Mr. Rabbit's stories were always interesting, even when doubtful, and besides—

Mr. Rabbit didn't wait for Mr. 'Possum to get done. He said it was one of those conversations that could be finished any time and didn't need any audience. "Perhaps Mr. 'Possum wouldn't mind waiting," he said, until the others had told their stories and gone home. Then he went right on to tell *his* story, like this:

"The sky is also a world—as big a world as this is, with a wide, rounding floor that looks blue in the daytime and nearly black at night, when the sun is gone. The sky country is really kind of an up-stairs world, and the stars are small windows, or peep-holes, in the big, blue floor, for the people up there to look down through when they want to see what is going on below. Those little windows are always there, day and night, though you can't see them in the daytime, because then the sun is shining here and not up there. In the evening, when it quits shining here, it goes up there, and then, of course, all the star windows are lit up, just like a window in the Hollow Tree at night. I will tell you a story of the sky country and its star windows, which explains everything. It has come down in our family ever since my folks lived in the moon, which was a great many great-grandfathers back, and is true, accordingly."

"The moon, where we used to live, is a pretty small world, compared with the sky world—being about like a pea compared with a bread-bowl —and our people used to have such big families that if they hadn't found some place for them to go they would have got so thick that the moon wouldn't have begun to hold them.

"Well, the moon is pretty close to the sky—not as close as you would think to look at it, for it seems right against it; it is really about a mile off —a mile and ten feet, exactly, I believe, or at least that was the length of my eighty-second great-grandfather's ladder, though, of course, that had to slant some. My grandparent built that ladder when our folks got together and decided that we were getting too thick and something must be done about it. My ancestor said the sky was just the thing. He had never been there, but he had a beautiful imagination, and he told them all about the lovely rivers and meadows and fields of clover they would find there, and said he would invent a way to get there for all who wanted to go.

"Everybody that heard my ancestor went home and told what a grand place the sky was, and made it even better than he had said; and some went around getting other crowds together and telling them about it, and went on improving the scenery until nobody had ever dreamed before of such a wonderful place as that sky-country, and it looked as if all the people in the moon were just waiting to climb Grandpaw's ladder as soon as it was done.

"It took my ancestor a good while to make it. The first time he got it done it was too short. When he sent out bids to the raising, and a lot of the neighbors came over to help, and ever so many folks were there with their things, ready to go up, they found it wouldn't touch by a good deal, and Grandpaw had to splice on about a quarter of a mile more. Then they had another raising, and when they got the ladder up and well propped, Grandpaw went up first to saw out a door to get in by.

"Now Grandpaw was smart. He knew that there are a lot of people never satisfied with anything, and who always want to come back, no matter how fine the place is. So he sawed out a little double trap, opening in the center, just big enough for single file, and put on strong spring hinges that open only one way—the way in, of course—with no handholds on the above side. Then he took a little look inside himself, and came back down the ladder, and the procession started.

"No such a collection of our family was ever seen before or since. Everybody in the moon had heard about that wonderful new country where there was lots of room and everything free, and they wanted to see it. They piled up that ladder in a steady stream for nearly a month before the line began to thin out, and it was a great help to the space on the moon. Of course none of them could come back to tell how it was there, or draw back once he got started through Grandpaw's spring-closing, one-way door. One long, thin rabbit called Snoop, who was always trying to see everything in advance, tried to jerk back after he got his head through, but Grandpaw's door caught him just back of the ears, and he decided to go on in. I don't know what my eighty-second great-grandfather saw when he took that first look. He didn't say. Grandpaw didn't join the sky procession himself, because he said he had to keep his ladder in repair. I forgot to say that he charged for each one that went up, and prospered a good deal, at first. When the crowd thinned out he sent several different ones around to explain what a grand place the sky was, and all about his ladder. My ancestor was a great hand to keep things moving.

"Well, by and by our folks who had stayed on the moon began to notice bright lights in the sky at night, and wondered what they were, and one night when business wasn't very good Grandpaw went about two-thirds of the way up his ladder to see. When he came back he said that those were windows of various sizes which the sky settlers were cutting through the floor so they could see what was going on back home. At first there were only a few scattering holes, but every night there were a lot more, until it looked as if those people up there put in all their time looking down at the place where they came from. Our folks used to listen to see if they wouldn't call down something about how they liked it, but nothing of that kind ever happened. Perhaps it was too far, or maybe they had made some law about it. Anyway, all that my people ever knew about those travelers was the windows they kept cutting, and those got so thick, by and by, that my ancestor was worried for fear the floor would get weak and the sky-world fall to pieces and spoil his income. So he sent up word by some who were going that if that window-cutting didn't stop he would take down his ladder and not let any more of their friends come. Very likely that scared them, for though the sky floor must have got pretty weak, it didn't come through and you see it is there, with all the windows, that we call stars, in it yet. The ladder built by my eighty-second great-grandfather remained in our family and was still working up to the time the moon tipped and spilt all that was left down here, just as I told you before. I never heard what became of it after that.

"As for those windows, I suppose they are still in use, as those sky-people would want to see what became of us. Those holes look pretty small, of course, from here, being so far away, and people got to calling them stars because they look like stars at this distance, though most of them would be round or square, I judge, if you could see them close. Some of them must have shutters, for sometimes there seem to be a great many more than others, especially on a very clear night, when I suppose those people up there have them all open. They are so thick then that I don't wonder my ancestor grew worried about the floor. I found a leaf, once, from one of Mr. Man's poetry books, and it said on it,

The night has a thousand eyes

and I suppose that meant the stars, but it must have been written a long time ago, for there are a good many more than a thousand now; and there's a verse in our family which says,

A million windows in the sky
Watch the nights and days go by.

"Which proves they have been there a long time and that they are really windows, and useful, and not mere ornaments, though they are certainly very pretty to look at, especially on a night like this and in such good company."

Then Mr. 'Possum said that he thought Mr. Rabbit's story was a very good one and explained the stars fully as well, in some ways, as Mr. 'Coon's story, though it was less exciting. He said he was sorry there was no story in his family to tell what the stars were, and asked Mr. Crow if there was anything of the kind in his family.

Mr. Crow said that there was a story, but that it wasn't exactly in his *family*—it was in *him*. Both Mr. 'Coon's and Mr. Rabbit's stories had been very good, he said, and no doubt true enough as far as they went, but that his story went farther, a good deal farther, especially in the direction of personal experience, even than Mr. 'Coon's. It had all been quite sad at the time, and he had never told it before to any one, but if they cared to hear it he would tell it now.

Then the 'Coon and the 'Possum and Mr. Jack Rabbit said they would be glad to hear a story from Mr. Crow, especially to-night; and Mr. Crow said he must think a little to get the beginning straight, which he did, and was ready presently to start.

MR. CROW'S STAR STORY

MR. CROW GIVES HIS ACCOUNT OF

HOW THE STARS WERE MADE

This is the story that Mr. Crow told on the night that he and Mr. 'Coon and Jack Rabbit and Mr. 'Possum sat on the edge of the world and hung their feet over the Big Nowhere and looked at the stars.

"Well," said Mr. Crow, "I can tell you something about the stars that may surprise you. I made the stars myself—not all of them, of course, but a good many of them. No doubt a number of them were made in the way Jack Rabbit has explained, and others in the way that Mr. 'Coon saw himself, and told us about, but most of the bright stars, and where there are a number together, I can account for, because I made them myself, as I said—though I did not enjoy it. They came out of my head—that is, they were knocked out—not all at once, but at different times. I did not make them alone—I had help—my wife helped me; also my mother-in-law, who was visiting us. It was this way:

"I was quite young when I married and I did not pick out the right person for a peaceful home. Minerva, which was her name, had never been brought up to do anything but go about with her mother and get up meetings on one thing and another and talk to them as long as they would stand it, and then go home and talk to Minerva's father, who was not very strong, and passed away at one such time. It was my turn after that. I came along just in time to take his place.

"It was nice enough at first. I thought how smart Mother Crow and Minerva were, and was proud when I saw them get up those big meetings. You never saw such meetings as those were. I've seen the trees in every direction black with our family, listening to Minerva and her mother talk. I don't know what they said—I never could seem to get the run of it, and, besides, I had to slip home early and get the supper, so I never got to hear their closing remarks, which might have explained things. Once when I asked Minerva to tell me in a few simple words what she had been talking about at the meeting, it seemed to fret her, and she said I seemed to understand private cooking better than public questions, and had better stick to it; which I did, after that, and I didn't go to the meetings at all. Minerva was not a cook herself, though her mother had been before she took to society work, and she told me some very good recipes.

"It was trying to learn those recipes that started my work in the star-making line. She gave me a recipe for chicken-pie one morning before she and Minerva started out, and the last thing she said, just before she left, was that it was only to have one crust. I had never made a pie that way. I always used two crusts—one above and one below, so when it came to that part this time, I put a lower crust in the pan, and then the chicken, and baked it just so, though I thought it would look much better with a top crust. When Mrs. Crow and Minerva came home, they were cross, and fussing a good deal at each other, because, for some reason, the meeting hadn't gone well, and when they came in and Mother Crow saw the open pie on the table, she asked me what I meant by making such a looking thing as that. I told her I had put on only one crust, according to her orders, and I thought, myself, a top crust would make it look better.

"Well, she didn't say another word. She just wheeled and gave me a clip on the left ear, and right then I saw three stars, just as plain as anything, fly out of my head and start for the sky. I don't know which ones they are, but they would be as big as any up there. When I got my balance I said that I could see that a pie made in that way was a mistake, though it would improve the looks of the sky; and Minerva and her mother both said I had gone crazy, and I had to dodge in two directions to keep from adding several more stars that same evening.

"I made plenty of them after that. They kept me busy at it. Something had gone wrong with their meetings, and they took it out on me. From what they said to each other I judged that some other ladies were holding still bigger meetings; also that those ladies were a disgrace, and that something ought to be done to them. Then all the things they thought about doing to those rival creatures they did to me, and I was in the star business most of the time. I made big ones and I made little ones, according to how mad my folks were and the aim they took. Also groups of stars: Once Minerva cracked me with the soup-ladle, and I made the dipper. I knew they were real stars, because every clear night when I went out for a little peace I could see new ones, and I could recognize which were mine.

"I don't know how many stars I made, nor what they all were now, but if I had kept on the sky would be running over by this time. I suppose I should have gone on, too, if something hadn't happened to Minerva. One day she went with her mother to attend one of those meetings which those creatures were holding over in the Burnt Deadening where there was a lot of bare, dead trees, and Minerva and Mother Crow tried to break it up.

"I didn't recognize my mother-in-law when she came home. She could only see a little out of one eye and there wasn't a whole feather on her. Minerva didn't come at all. Her funeral was next day, and then, of course, I was a widower, though not yet entirely out of the star business.

"Mrs. Crow gave up public life and started a boarding-house, as you may still remember, and I was with her a good while, and almost every day added a few stars to the firmament, as Mr. Dog calls it. Once she flung the milk-pitcher at my head, and when it hit and broke, it seemed to add some to the Milky Way. Several of those fancy designs up there I can remember making. They are all pretty enough to look at now, but I did not enjoy them much when I first saw them. I don't care to make any more, and, besides, there are plenty already. Sometimes I seem to see a few new ones up there, and it makes me think that somebody else has gone into the business of making them, the same way I did. I hope not, for though it may be the best and quickest way, it is not the one I should ever pick for myself again."

Mr. Crow sighed and lit his pipe, and everybody looked up at the twinkling sky. And Mr. 'Possum said he could understand now why there were several different kinds of stars. They had been made in different ways. Mr. 'Coon had seen Mr. Man working at one or two kinds; Mr. Rabbit's people had made another kind; and Mr. Crow had, perhaps, made several kinds. He said he had never heard anything so interesting in his life, or so reasonable.

MR. JACK RABBIT BRINGS A FRIEND

I

A NEW ARRIVAL IN THE BIG

DEEP WOODS TELLS A STORY

Once upon a time Mr. Jack Rabbit gave the Hollow Tree people a real surprise. It was a pleasant spring evening, and the 'Coon and 'Possum and the Old Black Crow were sitting outside after supper, and somebody had just remarked that it was a good while since they had seen Jack Rabbit, when Mr. Rabbit himself happened along and, for the first time they could remember, brought somebody with him. Then everybody jumped up, of course, to say, "Good evening," and Jack Rabbit said:

"This is a new friend I have made—possibly a distant relative, as we seem to belong to about the same family, though, of course, it doesn't really make any difference. Her name is Myrtle—Miss Myrtle Meadows —and she has had a most exciting, and very strange, and really quite awful adventure. I have brought her over because I know you will all be glad to hear about it. I have never heard anything so wonderful as the way she tells it."

Mr. Rabbit looked at Miss Meadows, and Miss Meadows tried to look at Jack Rabbit, but was quite shy and modest at being praised before everybody in that way. Then Mr. 'Coon brought her a nice little low chair, and she sat down, and they all asked her to tell about her great adventure, because they said they were tired of hearing their own old stories told over and over, and nearly always in the same way, though Mr. 'Possum could change his some when he tried. So then Miss Myrtle began to tell her story, but kept looking down at her lap at first, being so bashful among such perfect strangers as the Hollow Tree people were to her at that time.

"Well," she said, "I wasn't born in the Big Deep Woods, nor in any woods at all, but in a house with a great many more of our family, a long way from here, and owned by a Mr. Man who raised us to sell."

When Miss Myrtle said that the 'Coon and 'Possum and the Old Black Crow took their pipes out of their mouths and looked at her with very deep interest. They had once heard from Mr. Dog about menageries, [7] where Deep Woods people and others were kept for Mr. Man and his friends to look at, but they had never heard of a place where any of their folks were raised to sell. Mr. 'Possum was just going to ask a question—probably as to how they were fed—when Mr. Rabbit said, "'Sh!" and Miss Meadows went on:

"It was quite a nice place, and we were pretty thick in the little house, which was a good deal like a cage, with strong wires in front, though it had doors, too, to shut us in when it rained or was cold. Mr. Man, or some of his family, used to bring us fresh grass and clover and vegetables to eat, every day, and sometimes would open a door and let us out for a short time on the green lawn. We never went far, or thought of running away, but ran in, pretty soon, and cuddled down, sometimes almost in a pile, we were so thick; and we were all very happy indeed.

"But one day Mr. Man came to our house and opened the door and reached in and lifted several of us out—about twenty or so, I should think—one after another, by the ears—and put us into a flat box with slats across the top, and said, 'Now you little chaps are going to have a trip and see something.' I didn't know what he meant, but I can see now, that he didn't mean nearly so much as happened—not in *my* case. A number of my brothers and sisters were in the box with me, and though we were quite frightened, we were excited, too, for we wondered where we were going, and what wonderful things we should see."

Miss Myrtle paused and wiped her eyes with a handkerchief that looked very much like one of Jack Rabbit's; then she said:

"I suppose I shall never know what became of all the others of our poor little broken family, and I know they are wondering what became of me, but of course there is no way to find out now, and Mr. Jack Rabbit says I must try to forget and be happy.

"Well, Mr. Man put the box into a wagon and we rode and rode, and were so frightened, for we had never done such a thing before, and by and by we came to a very big town—a place with ever so many houses and all the Mr. Mans and their families in the world, I should think, and so much noise that we all lay flat and tried to bury our heads, to keep from being made deaf. By and by Mr. Man stopped and took our box from the wagon, and another Mr. Man stepped out of a place that I learned later was a kind of store where they sell things, and the new Mr. Man took our box and set it in front of his store, and put a card on it with some words that said, 'For Sale,' and threw us in some green stuff to eat, and there we were, among ever so many things that we had never seen before.

"Well, it was not very long until a tall Mr. Man and his little boy stopped and looked at us, and Mr. Store Man came out and lifted up the cover of our box and held us up, one after the other, by the ears, until he came to Tip, one of my brothers who wasn't very smart, but was quite good-looking and had a tuft of white on his ears which made him have that name. Mr. Man's boy said he would take Tip, and Tip giggled and was so pleased because he had been picked first. Mr. Store Man put him in a big paper bag, and that was the last we saw of Tip. I hope he did not have the awful experience I had, though, of course, everything is all right now," and Miss Myrtle looked at Jack Rabbit, who looked at Miss Myrtle and said that no harm should come to her ever again.

"Smut was next to go—a nice little chap with a blackish nose. A little girl of Mr. Man's bought him, and it was another little girl that bought me. She looked at all of us a good while, and pretty soon she happened to see that I was looking at her, and she said she could see in my eyes that I was asking her to take me, which was so, and pretty soon I was in a bag, too, and when the little girl opened the bag I was in her house—a very fine place, with a number of wonderful things in it besides her family, and plenty to eat—much more than I wanted, though I had a good appetite, being young.

"I was very lonesome, though, for there were none of the Rabbit family there, and I had nobody to talk to, or cuddle up to at night. I had a little house all to myself, butoften through the day my little girl would hold me and stroke my fur, trying as hard as she could to make me happy and enjoy her society.

"I really did enjoy it, too, sometimes, when she did not squeeze me too hard, which she couldn't help, she was so fond of me. When I would sit up straight and wash my face, as I did every morning, she would call everybody to see me, and said I was the dearest thing in the world."

When Miss Meadows said that Jack Rabbit looked at her with his head tipped a little to one side, as if he were trying to decide whether Mr. Man's little girl had been right or not. Then he looked at the Hollow Tree people and said:

"H'm! H'm! Very nice little girl" (meaning Mr. Man's, of course), "and very smart, too."

"I got used to being without my own folks," Miss Meadows went on, "but I did not forget the nice green grass of the country, and always wanted to go back to it. If I had known what was going to happen to me in the country I should not have been so anxious to get there.

"I had been living with that little girl and her family about a month, I suppose, when one day she came running to my house and took me out, and said:

"'Oh, Brownie'—that was her name for me—'we are going to the country, Brownie dear, where you can run and play on the green grass, and eat fresh clover, and have the best time.'

"Well, of course I was delighted, and we did go to the country, but I did not have the best time—at least, not for long.

"It was all right at the start. We went in Mr. Man's automobile. I had never seen one before, and it was very scary at first. I was in a box on the back seat with Mr. Man's little girl and her mother, and I stood up most of the time, and looked over the top of the box at the world going by so fast that it certainly seemed to be turning around, as I once heard the little girl say it really did. When we began to come to the country I saw the grass and woods and houses, all in a whirl, and the little girl helped me so I could see better, and my heart beat so fast that I thought it was going to tear me to pieces. I felt as if I must jump out and run away, but she held me very tight, and by and by I grew more peaceful.

"We got there that evening, and it was a lovely place. There was a large lawn of grass, and some big trees, and my little girl let me run about the lawn, though I was still so scared that I wanted to hide in every good place I saw. So she put me in a pretty new house that had a door, and wire net windows to look out of, and then set the little house out in the yard and gave me plenty of fresh green food, and I was just getting used to everything when the awful thing happened.

"It happened at night, the worst time, of course, for terrible things, and they generally seem to come then. It was such a pleasant evening that my little girl thought it would be well for me to stay in my house outside, instead of having me in the big house, which she thought I did not care for, and that was true, though I can see now that the big house would have been safer at such a time.

"So I stayed in my little house out on the terrace, and thought how pleasant it was out there, and nibbled some nice carrot tops she had put in for me, and watched the lights commence to go out in the big house, and saw my little girl come to the window and look out at me, and then her light went out, too, and pretty soon I suppose I must have gone to sleep."

II

MISS MYRTLE MEADOWS CONTINUES

HER ADVENTURES

"Really, I don't know what time it was that I woke up, but I know I did not wake up naturally. I just seemed to jump out of my sleep, and I was wide awake in a second. Something was clawing and scratching at one of my wire windows, and then I saw two big, fiery eyes, and knew it was some fierce creature, and that it was after me. Well, I thought I had been scared before in my short life, but I could see now that I had never really known what it was to be scared. I didn't see how I could live from one minute to the next, I was in such a state, and I couldn't move hand or foot.

"I knew what it was after me. Our Mr. Man had a big old Mr. Dog that I had seen looking at me very interestedly once before when my little girl carried my house past him. They kept him fastened with a chain, but somehow he had worked himself loose, and now he had come to make a late supper out of poor defenseless me. I would have talked to him, and tried to shame him out of it, but I was too scared even to speak, for he was biting and clawing at that wire net window as hard as he could, and I could see that it was never going to keep him out, for it was beginning to give way, and all of a sudden it did give way, and his big old head came smashing right through into my house, and I expected in another second to be dead.

"But just in that very second I seemed to come to life. I didn't have anything to do with it at all. My legs suddenly turned into springs and sent me flying out under old Mr. Dog's neck, between his fore feet; then they turned into wings, and if I touched the ground again for at least three miles I don't remember it. I could hear old Mr. Dog back there, and I could tell by his language that he was mad. He thought he was chasing me, but he wasn't. He was just wallowing through the bushes and across a boggy place that I had sailed over like a bird. If he could have seen how fast I was going he would have thought he was standing still. But he was old and foolish, and kept blundering along, until I couldn't hear him any more, he was so far behind. Then, by and by, it was morning, and I *really* came to life and found I was tired and hungry and didn't know in the least where I was.

"There didn't seem to be anything to eat there, either, but only leaves and woods; and I was afraid to taste such green things as I saw, because they were wild and might make me sick. So I went on getting more tired and hungry and lost, and was nearly ready to give up when I heard some one call, just overhead, and I looked up, and saw a friendly-looking bird who said his name was Mr. Robin, and asked if there was anything he could do for me. When I told him how tired and hungry I was, he came down and showed me some things I could eat without danger, and invited me home with him. He said I was in the Big Deep Woods, and that there was a vacant room in the tree where he and Mrs. Robin had their nest and I could stay there as long as I liked.

"So I went home with Mr. Robin, and Mrs. Robin was ever so kind, and said she thought I must be of the same family as Mr. Jack Rabbit, because we resembled a good deal, and sent over for him right away. I was ever so glad to think I was going to see one of my own folks again, and when Mr. Rabbit came we sat right down, and I told him my story, and we tried to trace back and see what relation we were, but it was too far back, and besides, I was too young when I left home to know much about my ancestors. Mr. Rabbit said if we were related at all it must be through his mother, as she was very handsome, and he thought I looked like her a good deal. He said what a fine thing it was that I had quit being a house rabbit and had decided to be a wild, free rabbit in the Big Deep Woods, though, of course, it was really old Mr. Dog who decided it for me, and I was quite sorry to leave my little girl, who was always so good to me and loved me very much. It makes me sad when I remember how I saw her at the window, that last time, but I don't think I want to go back, anyway, now since Jack—Mr. Rabbit, I mean—is teaching me all about Deep Woods life and says he is not going to let me go back at all—ever!"

Little Miss Myrtle all at once seemed very much embarrassed again, and looked down into her lap, and Mr. Jack Rabbit seemed quite embarrassed, too, when he tried to say something, because he had to cough two or three times before he could get started.

"H'm! H'm!" he said. "Now that you have all heard Miss Meadows's wonderful story, and what a narrow escape she had—an escape which those present can understand, for all of us have had close calls in our time—I am sure you will be glad to hear that the little stranger has consented to remain in the Big Deep Woods and share such of the Deep Woods fortunes as I can provide for her. In fact—I may say—h'm! that—h'm!—Miss Meadows a week from to-day is to become—h'm!—Mrs. Jack Rabbit."

Then all the Hollow Tree people jumped right up and ran over to shake hands with Mr. Rabbit and Miss Myrtle Meadows, and Mr. 'Possum said they must have a big wedding, because big weddings always meant good things to eat, and that everybody must come, and that he would show them how a wedding was to be enjoyed. Mr. Crow promised to cook his best things, and Mr. 'Coon said he would think up some performances for the guests to do, and then everybody began to talk about it, until it was quite late before Jack Rabbit and Miss Meadows walked away toward Mr. Robin's, calling back, "Good night!" to their good friends of the Hollow Tree.

MR. RABBIT'S WEDDING

I

THE HOLLOW TREE PEOPLE GATHER

TO CELEBRATE A GREAT EVENT

"Well, you remember that I told you about Mr. Jack Rabbit and Miss Myrtle Meadows, and the wedding they had planned," says the Story Teller one pleasant afternoon when he and the Little Lady have been taking a long walk and are resting in the shade in the very edge of the Big Deep Woods.

The Little Lady nods. "But you never told me about the wedding," she says, "and I want to hear about that more than anything. They *had* a wedding, didn't they?—the Hollow Tree people were going to get it up, you know."

"Well, they did; and there was never such a wedding in the Big Deep Woods. This was the way it was":

Mr. 'Possum began to plan right away all the things that Mr. Crow was to cook, and went out every night to help bring in something, though Mr.

'Possum is not a great hand for work, in general, except when somebody else does it. Mr. 'Coon went right to work on the program of things to be done at the wedding, and decided to have a regular circus, where everybody in the Big Deep Woods could show what he could do best, or what he used to do best when he was young. Every little while Jack Rabbit and Miss Meadows walked over to talk about it, and by and by they came over and wrote out all the invitations, which Mr. Robin promised to deliver, though he had once made a big mistake with an invitation by having a hole in his pocket.[8]

But Mr. Robin didn't make any mistake this time, and went around from place to place, and stopped to talk a little with each one, because he is friends with everybody. Mr. Redfield Bear and Mr. Turtle and Mr. Squirrel and Mr. Dog and Mr. Fox all said they would come, and would certainly bring something for the happy couple, for it wasn't every day that one got a chance to attend such a wedding as Jack Rabbit's would be; and everybody remembered how the bride had come to the Deep Woods in that most romantic and strange way, after having been brought up with Mr. Man's people, and all wanted to know what she looked like, and if she spoke with much accent, and what she was going to wear, and if Mr. Robin thought she would be satisfied to stay in the Deep Woods, which must seem a great change; and if she had a pleasant disposition. They knew, of course, Mr. Robin would be apt to know about most of those things, because she had been staying at his house ever since that awfulnight when she escaped from old Mr. Dog.

Mr. Robin said he had never known any one with a sweeter nature than Miss Myrtle's, and that old Mr. Dog's loss had been the Big Deep Woods' gain. Then he told them as much as he knew about the wedding, and what each one was expected to do, as a performance, and hurried home to help Mrs. Robin, who was as busy as she could be, getting the bride's outfit ready and teaching her something about housekeeping, though Jack Rabbit, who had been a bachelor such a long time, would know a number of things, too.

Well, they decided to have the wedding out under some big trees by the Race Track, because that would give a good, open place for the performances, which everybody was soon practising. Mr. Crow was especially busy, because he was going to show how he used to fly. Every morning he was out there very early, running and flapping about, and every afternoon he was cooking, right up to the day of the wedding.

Mr. 'Possum was up himself, *that* morning, almost before daylight, going around and looking at all the things Mr. Crow had cooked, tasting a little of most of them, though he had already tasted of everything at least seven times while the cooking was going on; and he said that if there was one thing in the world that would tempt him to get married it was having a wedding given him such as Mr. Rabbit's was going to be.

Then when Mr. Crow and Mr. 'Coon had snatched a cup of coffee and a bite they all gathered up the fine cakes and chicken pies and puddings and things and started for the Race Track, for the wedding was going to begin pretty early and last all day.

It looked a little cloudy in the morning, but it cleared up before long, and was as fine a June day as anybody could ask for. As soon as the Hollow Tree people came they put down their things and began practising their performances for the last time. Mr. Crow said if he was going to do his old flying trick it was well that he had one more try at it; then he got in light flying costume and started from a limb, and did pretty well for any one that had been out of practice so long; and he could even rise from the ground by going out on the Race Track and taking a running start. Then, by and by, Mr. Redfield Bear came along, bringing a box of fine maple sugar for the young couple, and Mr. Fox came with a brand-new feather bed, and Mr. Squirrel brought a big nut cake which Mrs. Squirrel had made, and sent ahead by *him* because she might be a little late, on account of the children.

Then Jack Rabbit himself came with the finest clothes on they had ever seen him wear, and with a beautiful bouquet, and carrying a new handkerchief and a pair of gloves and a cane. Everybody stood right up when he walked in, and said they had never seen him look so young and handsome and well-dressed; and Mr. Rabbit bowed and said, "To be happy is to be young—to be young is to be handsome—to be handsome is to be well-dressed." Then everybody said that besides all those things Jack Rabbit was certainly the smartest person in the Big Deep Woods.

And just then Mr. and Mrs. Robin arrived with the bride, and when the Deep Woods people saw her they just clasped their hands and couldn't say a word, for she took their breath quite away.

Miss Meadows was almost overcome, too, with embarrassment, and was looking down at the ground, so she didn't see who was there at first; but when she happened to look up and saw Mr. Bear she threw up her arms and would have fallen fainting if Jack Rabbit hadn't caught her, for she had never seen such a large, fierce-looking Deep Woods person before. But Jack Rabbit told her right away that this was not any of the Savage Bear family, but Cousin Redfield, one of the Brownwood Bears, who had been friendly a long time with all Deep Woods people, and he showed her the nice present Mr. Bear had brought. So then she thanked Cousin Redfield Bear very prettily, though she looked as if she might fly into Jack Rabbit's arms at any moment.

She did more than that presently, though not on Mr. Bear's account. Everybody was busy getting things ready when in walked Mr. Dog, all dressed up and with a neat package in his hand.

Well, nobody had thought to tell Miss Meadows about this *good* Mr. Dog who lived with Mr. Man in the edge of the Deep Woods and had been friendly with the Hollow Tree people so long, and when everybody said, "Why, here's Mr. Dog! How do you do, Mr. Dog?" she whirled around and then gave a wild cry and made the longest leap the Hollow Tree people had ever seen—they said so, afterward—and never stopped to faint, but dashed away, and Jack Rabbit would have stayed a bachelor if she hadn't tripped in her wedding-gown; though Jack was in time to catch her before she fell, which saved her dress from damage. Then Mr. Rabbit explained to her all about this Mr. Dog, and coaxed her back, and Mr. Dog made his best bow and offered his present—a nice, new cook-book which somebody had sent to Mrs. Man, who said she didn't want it, because she had her old one with a great many of her own recipes written in. He said he thought it was just the thing for the bride to start new with, and she would, of course, add her own recipes, too, in time. Mr. Crow said he would give her some of his best ones, right away, especially the ones for the things he had brought to-day, which ought to be eaten now, pretty soon, while they were fresh. So that reminded them all of the wedding, and Miss Meadows thanked Mr. Dog for his handsome and useful present, and just then Mr. Turtle came in, bringing some beautiful bridal wreaths he had promised to make, and right behind him was Mr. Owl, who is thought to be wise, and is Doctor and Preacher and Lawyer in the Big Deep Woods, and performs all the ceremonies.

So then everybody had come, and there was nothing to wait for, and Mr. Jack Rabbit led Miss Meadows out in the center of the nice shade, and Mr. Owl stood before them, and all the other Deep Woods people arranged themselves in a circle except Mr. and Mrs. Robin, who stood by the bride and groom.

Then Mr. Owl said, "Are all present?"

And everybody said, "All present who have been invited."

Then Mr. Owl said, "Who gives this bride away?"

"I do," said Mr. Robin, "though she isn't really mine, because I only happened to find her one morning when—"

Mr. Robin was going on to explain all about it, but Mr. Owl said, "'Sh!" and went right on:

"Mr. Jack Rabbit, Mr. Robin gives you Miss Myrtle Meadows to love and cherish and obey, and Mr. Dog has brought a cook-book, and Mr. Bear some maple sugar, and all the others have brought good things. The wedding-feast is therefore waiting. What is left will be yours. Let us hope there will still be the cook-book, but Miss Myrtle Meadows will not be with us, for I now pronounce her to be Mrs. Jack Rabbit, and may you be happy as long as possible, and longer."

Then everybody became suddenly excited and pushed up to congratulate Mr. and Mrs. Rabbit, and when the bride heard herself called "Mrs. Jack

Rabbit" she was more embarrassed than ever, and couldn't get used to it for at least two minutes. Then they all sat down and ate and ate, and Mr. 'Possum said he never felt so romantic in his life, which was all he did say, except, "Please pass the chicken pie," or, "A little more gravy, please."

Well, when they had all had about enough, except Mr. 'Possum, who was still taking a taste of this and a bite of that, where things were in reach, Mr. Rabbit got up and said he had written a little something for the occasion, and if they cared to hear it he would read it now.

So then they all said, "Read it! Read it!" and Jack Rabbit stood up very nice and straight, and read:

BEGINNING ANEW

I've lived alone a long, long time,
And frequently the days seemed blue,
But now they all are bright, for I'm
Beginning anew.

My friends live in the Big Deep Woods
And they, I know, are happy, too,
To see me with my household goods,
Beginning anew.

Oh, fair Miss Meadows, now no more,
Though surely not with heart less true,
As lovely Mrs. Rabbit, you're
Beginning anew.

II

THE GREAT PERFORMANCE THAT

FOLLOWED THE WEDDING DINNER

When Mr. Rabbit finished everybody applauded and he made a nice bow, though he said that in the last stanza there was an imperfect rhyme which he hoped they would excuse for the sake of the great feeling in it; and everybody said, "Yes, yes," and then when they were quiet Mr. 'Coon rose and said that now the program of performances would begin, and that it would open and close with flying exhibitions—the first by Mr. and Mrs. Robin, and the last by Mr. Crow, who, though a good deal out of practice, had promised to give them a sample of old-fashioned flying.

Everybody cheered, of course, and then Mr. and Mrs. Robin suddenly sprang up into the air and began circling around and around and darting over and under, in the very prettiest way, and so fast that it almost made one dizzy to watch them. Sometimes they would seem to be standing straight up, facing each other for a few seconds, then they would whirl over and over in regular somersaults, suddenly darting high up in the air, sailing down, at last, in a regular spiral, and landing on the grass right in front of the bride and groom.

Then all clapped their hands and said it was the most wonderful thing ever seen, and Mr. Crow said if he should try to fly like that he would never know afterward whether his head was on right or not.

Then Mr. 'Coon rose to remark that Mr. Fox was next on the program and would give a little exhibition in light and fancy running.

Mr. Fox, who hadn't eaten as much dinner as he might, because he wanted to be in good trim for his performance, got right up and with a leap landed out on the Race Track, and then for the next five minutes they could hardly tell whether he was running or flying, he leaped so lightly and skipped so swiftly, his fine, bushy tail waving like a beautiful, graceful plume that seemed to guide him this way and that and to be just the thing for Mr. Fox's purpose.

Mr. Fox was applauded, too, when he sat down, and so was Mr. Squirrel, who came next, and showed that *his* bushy tail was also useful, for he gave a leaping exhibition from one limb to another, and leaped farther and farther each time, until they thought he would surely injure himself; but he never did and he got as much applause as Mr. Fox when he finally landed right in front of the bride and groom and made a neat bow.

Then Mr. Turtle gave a heavy-weight carrying exhibition, and let all get on his back that could stick on, and walked right down the same Race Track where so long before he had run the celebrated race with Mr. Hare, and said when he came back he felt just as young and able to-day as he had then, and was much stronger in the shell.

Cousin Redfield Bear danced. Nobody thought he was going to do that. They thought he would likely give a climbing exhibition, or something of the kind. But he didn't—he danced. And if you could have seen Cousin Redfield dance, with his arms akimbo, and his head thrown back, and watch him cut the pigeon-wing, you would have understood why he wanted to do it. He knew it would amuse them and make them want to dance, too; which it did, and pretty soon they were in a circle around him, bride and groom and all, dancing around and around and singing the Hollow Tree song, which all the Deep Woods people know.

They danced until they were tired, and then it was Mr. Dog's turn to do something. Mr. Dog said he couldn't fly, though certainly he would like to; and he couldn't run like Mr. Fox, or jump like Mr. Squirrel, or make poetry like Mr. Rabbit, or dance like Mr. Bear—though once, a long time ago, as some of them might remember, he had taken a dancing-lesson from Jack Rabbit.[9] He couldn't do any of those things as well as the others, he said, so he would just make a little speech called:

MR. MAN

"Mr. Man is my friend, and we live together. He is always my friend, though you might not suspect it, sometimes, the things he says to me. But he is, and I am Mr. Man's friend, through thick and thin.

"I am also the friend, now, of the Deep Woods people, and expect to remain so, because I have learned to know them and they have learned to know me. That is the trouble about the Deep Woods people and Mr. Man. They don't know each other. The Deep Woods people think that Mr. Man is after them, and there is some truth in it, because Mr. Man thinks the Deep Woods people are after him, or his property, when, of course, all Deep Woods people know that it was never intended that Mr. Man should own all the chickens, and they are obliged to borrow one, now and then, in order to have chicken pie, such as has been served on this happy occasion.

"I am looking forward to the day when Mr. Man will understand this, as well as the Hollow Tree people do, and will become friendly and open his heart and hen-house to all who would enter in."

Mr. Dog's speech made quite a sensation. Mr. 'Possum, especially, said it was probably the greatest speech of modern times, and was going on to say more when Mr. 'Coon whispered to him that it was their turn on the program. So then Mr. 'Coon and Mr. 'Possum got up, side by side, and Mr. 'Possum walked rather soggily, because he had eaten so much, though he managed to get up a little hickory tree and out on a smooth, straight limb while Mr. 'Coon climbed up another, a few feet away. Then all at once Mr. 'Possum dropped and held by his tail, which was hooked around the limb, and Mr. 'Coon dropped and held by his hands, and then began to swing; and pretty soon, when Mr. 'Coon was swung out nearly straight in Mr. 'Possum's direction, he let go and turned over in the air and caught Mr. 'Possum's hands, and they both swung, and everybody cheered and said that was the finest thing yet. Then they went right on swinging—Mr. 'Possum holding by his tail, until they got a good start, and pretty soon Mr. 'Possum gave Mr. 'Coon a big swing, expecting him to turn clear over and catch his own limb again. But Mr. 'Possum and Mr. 'Coon had both eaten a good deal, and Mr. 'Coon didn't get a very good start. He just missed the limb he was aimed at, and hit Mr. Fox's feather bed, which was lying right in front of Mr. and Mrs. Rabbit, along with other presents, all of which was a good thing for Mr. 'Coon. For Mr. 'Coon is pretty smart and quick to think. He jumped right up when everybody was laughing, and made a bow to Mr. and Mrs. Rabbit as if he had meant to land just that way, and everybody laughed still harder and enjoyed it more than anything. Then Mr. 'Possum swung up and caught his limb with his hands, but couldn't get back on it again, and called for the feather bed, which Mr. 'Coon and Mr. Fox brought, and Mr. 'Possum dropped on it like a sack of salt, and everybody enjoyed it more and more.

Well, it was Mr. Crow's turn then, and he said he would probably have to have the feather bed, too. But he went out on the open track and took a little run, and about the second time around spread out his big, black wings and lifted himself from the ground, not very high at first, and he had to flap pretty hard, but he kept getting a little higher all the time, and presently he swung about in a big circle, and went sailing and flapping around and around, up and up, until he was as high as the little trees, then as high as the big trees, then as high as a church steeple, and still kept going up until he looked small and black against the sky; and Mr. Robin whispered to Mrs. Robin that Mr. Crow might be old and out of practice, but *they* had never dared to fly as high as that, and said he didn't believe any of Mr. Crow's family had ever gone higher.

Mr. Crow was just a black speck, pretty soon, and everybody was getting rather scared, for they wondered what would happen to him if something about him should give way; and just when they were all watching and keeping quite still, they heard the most curious sound, that seemed to be coming nearer, getting louder and louder. At first nobody spoke, but just listened. Then Mr. 'Possum said something must have happened to Mr. Crow's machinery and he was coming down for repairs. And sure enough, they did see Mr. Crow coming down, about as fast as he could drive, making quick circles, and the noise was getting louder and louder, though it didn't seem to be Mr. Crow who was making it, for he never could make a sound like that, no matter what had happened to his works.

Mr. Crow came down a good deal faster than he went up, and in about five seconds more landed right among them, and they saw he was scared.

"Oh," he gasped, "we are all lost! The biggest bird in the world is coming to devour us! I saw it—it is making that terrible noise! It is as big as Mr. Man's house! It is as big as his yard! It is as big as the Big Deep Woods!"

And just then a great black shadow, like the shadow of a cloud, came right over them, and that noise got so loud it drowned everything, and when they looked—for they were too scared to run—sure enough, right above them was the biggest bird in the world—a thousand times bigger than Mr. Crow, of stranger shape than anything they had ever seen, and very terrible indeed. But all at once Mr. Dog gave a quick bark, which made them all jump—especially the bride—and shouted:

"It's all right—it's all right! I know what it is. I see a Mr. Man up there. It's a flying-machine; it's only passing over, and won't hurt us at all!"

And sure enough all the rest could see a Mr. Man up there, too, then; and Mr. Dog went on to tell them how he had seen some pictures of just such a machine in one of Mr. Man's picture papers, and that it was the great new invention by which Mr. Man could go around in the air like a bird, though probably not so well as Mr. and Mrs. Robin and Mr. Crow, and certainly with a good deal more noise.

Then the Deep Woods people were not afraid any more, and watched the flying-machine as long as they could see it, and when it was quite out of sight Mr. Rabbit made a little speech in which he said that if anything had been needed to make his grand wedding complete it was to have a performance given for it by Mr. Man, even though Mr. Man might not realize that he was entertaining a wedding. And everybody said, "Yes, yes, that's so," and that this was the greatest day in the Big Deep Woods, which I believe it really was.

Then they all formed a procession and marched to Jack Rabbit's house, to take home the bride and groom. As they marched they sang the Hollow Tree song, ending with the chorus:

Then here's to the friends of the Big Deep Woods,
And to theirs, wherever they be,

And here's to the Hollow, Hollow, Hollow, Hollow, Hollow,
And here's to the Hollow Tree.

THE END

FOOTNOTES:

[1]"Mr. Turtle's Thunder Story" in *The Hollow Tree and Deep Woods Book*.

[2]*Hollow Tree and Deep Woods Book*.

[3]*Hollow Tree Snowed-In Book*.

[4]See frontispiece.

[5]"Mr. Turtle's Thunder Story" in *The Hollow Tree and Deep Woods Book*.

[6]"On the Edge of the World," in *The Hollow Tree and Deep Woods Book*.

[7]"Mr. Dog at the Circus," in *The Hollow Tree Snowed-In Book*.

[8]"How Mr. Dog Got Even," *The Hollow Tree and Deep Woods Book*.

[9]"Mr. Dog Takes Lessons in Dancing," in *The Hollow Tree and Deep Woods Book*.

Made in the USA
San Bernardino, CA
25 June 2019